Booster Book
for Key Stage 2

Lawrie Ryan

Rosemary Sherrington

Published in 2003 by:
Nelson Thornes Ltd
Delta Place
27 Bath Road
CHELTENHAM
GL53 7TH
United Kingdom

03 04 05 06 07/ 10 9 8 7 6 5 4 3 2 1

A catalogue record for this book is available from the British Library

ISBN 0 7487 6869 6

Illustrations by Oxford Designers & Illustrators
Page make-up by Oxford Designers & Illustrators

Printed in Great Britain by Ashford Colour Press

Contents

Introduction

Science Attainment Target 1 (Sc1) remains the most important aspect of science at Key Stage 2. Building on the foundations established in Key Stage 1, the central role of scientific enquiry in learning about our world becomes more apparent to children. As their skills improve, they will experience the excitement that stems from planning their own enquiries and taking ownership of their own learning.

This book offers teachers a flexible resource that can be used to develop skills at different levels in a range of common enquiries tackled throughout Key Stage 2. The enquiries all feature in the QCA Scheme of Work, but extra guidance, especially with differentiation, is included in the notes for teachers that accompany each activity.

What's in the book?

A. Teacher's notes

Learning objectives

The learning objectives for each activity are listed at the start of an enquiry. The key features of those related to Sc1 skills are highlighted.

Lesson notes

These start with an approximate timing for the enquiry and define the type of enquiry the children will carry out. Based on work done by the AKSIS project, they can be designated:

- Fair tests (in which children change one factor, or variable, whilst keeping others the same)
- Biological enquiries (in which some factors are difficult to control, but the aim is to spot patterns; sample sizes are an important feature of these enquiries)
- Exploration (in which children can use their senses to observe things, sometimes over an extended period of time)
- Classification (in which children sort things into groups or identify things)
- Problem solving (in which children design solutions to a variety of problems, often technological)
- Research (in which children will consult secondary sources to answer their scientific questions)

This is followed by suggestions under the headings:

- Introduction   - Group work   - Whole class

Differentiated Sc1 learning outcomes

Learning outcomes are the key to accurate assessment, and with each enquiry you will find learning outcomes at a variety of levels.

The differentiated sheets

A brief outline of each sheet is given and a star system is used to give a quick guide to differentiation (★ sheets offer most support and ★★★ sheets provide most challenge). Levels are indicated where sheets closely match a Level Description from Sc1.

Background information

Information for teachers is provided on the skills developed in the enquiry and on the science upon which the activity is based. The Sc1 background will discuss differentiation in the skill and has been planned to show progression across the key stage.

B. Sc1 Sheets

There are three types of sheet to go with each enquiry:

Skill development practice sheets

These give children an opportunity to practise a skill developed in the enquiry. These can be done before the enquiry to help prepare children for their activity. Alternatively, they can be used retrospectively in the light of diagnostic assessment information gained as children tackle their enquiry.

Differentiated Sc1 support sheets

These form the main body of the sheets and offer support at a variety of levels of demand and are to be used as children carry out their enquiry. The teacher can match sheets to different individuals or groups.

Sc1 checklists

Children can use these sheets, with support where necessary, to record the aspects of the skill(s) they have performed in the course of their enquiry. Levels are included to aid teacher assessment of Sc1. These are based on the Level Descriptions whenever possible, but also include the authors' interpretation for finer differentiation.

Teeth and eating: What do our pets eat?

Nelson Thornes Ref: PS Kit 3.1.4

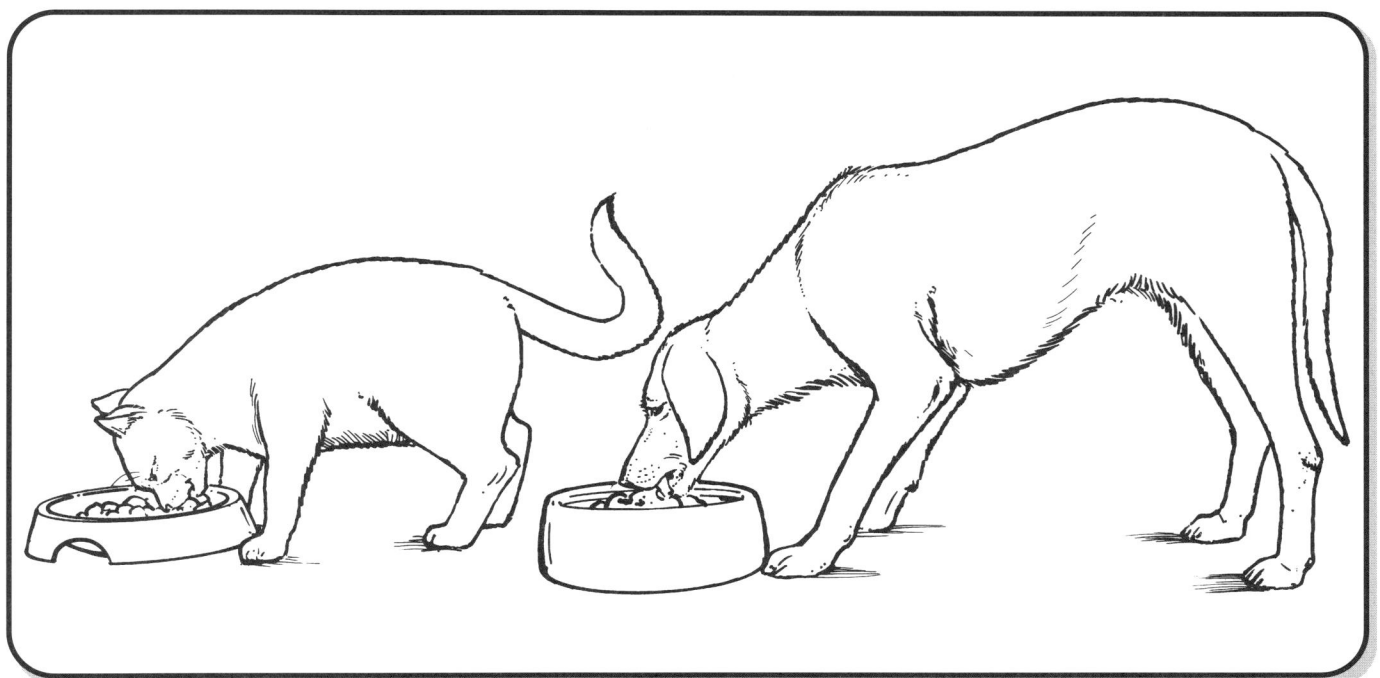

Learning objectives

Children should learn:

- to **turn ideas** about the diet of animals **into a form that can be investigated**
- to **decide how many** animals should be investigated **and the range** of foods to be considered
- to **present evidence** about the foods eaten by animals **in a suitable bar chart or pictogram**
- to **decide whether the evidence is sufficient to draw conclusions**.

Lesson notes

⏱ Approximate timing: 1.5 hours, plus some time at home asking about what pets eat.

Type of scientific enquiry

This scientific enquiry will give the children the opportunity to conduct a survey.

Introduction

Ask the children for their ideas from the previous lesson about the diet of their pets:

- Encourage the children to pose questions that could lead to a scientific enquiry.

- Discuss the children's suggestions and move them towards deciding on a question about cats' food.

Note: This is a good choice for an investigation because there are many people with cats; cats seem to have preferred foods, cat food tends to be of one sort or another and is easy to distinguish.

It is more scientific to consider the food rather than the manufacturer. Children who have no cat could call a friend, neighbour or relative.

Ask why it is important to survey as many cats as possible. Now turn this into a question that can be tested:

- What do cats eat?
- Which food do most cats eat?

Then make predictions:

'My cat only likes chicken, she won't touch any other food, so I predict that cats like chicken best'.
'And my cat likes chicken, but he eats anything we give him, so I don't know if you're right'.
'We don't give our cat fish, but she likes chicken. I think all cats like chicken'.

Organise the groups to collect data at home or use their own knowledge. Make large versions of Sheets 1 and 4.

Individual and group work

Discuss what the children have found out and how they have completed their tables. Show the children how to put their information onto the class pictogram or bar chart. Once they have started this, organise the groups to make their own charts of the group's data.

Help the children where necessary and question them to elicit and develop their understanding about the food most cats eat, conducting a survey, making charts and a simple analysis of the charts.

Whole class

Discuss the findings. Begin with the children's own work and ask individuals and groups to talk about what they found out. Move to the whole class chart. What do these results tell us? — Favourite/least favourite, how many, what proportion are in each category, any surprises.

● Is this different from your chart? In what ways?

● Is this evidence better? How is it better?

● Can we say which is cats' favourite food?

● How might the results be better if we... (ask the local supermarket to tell us which cat food they sell the most of?)

● Why are there more cats on the pictogram/bar charts than we surveyed?

● Why don't all cats eat fish/chicken...?

Differentiated Sc1 learning outcomes

Turning ideas into a form that can be investigated

● suggests questions
● listens to others' ideas
● considers/decides which is the best question to be investigated by whole class.

Deciding what evidence to collect

● decides which animal to survey
● decides the range of foods
● decides how much data to collect.

Presenting evidence in a bar chart or pictogram

● with help, draws cats on the pictogram
● draws cats appropriately on a pictogram
● with help, enters results on a class bar chart
● enters results on group and/or class bar chart
● designs their own chart and enters the group results.

Deciding whether the evidence is sufficient to draw conclusions

● says which food is eaten by most cats (is the favourite) on their own and the class bar chart
● knows that the class chart is the result of a larger sample
● knows that the larger the sample the better the evidence.

Using the differentiated sheets

Sheet 1★★★ is to give children practice in analysing a bar chart. They look at the results of a survey and are asked to draw a valid conclusion from the evidence on the bar chart. (Providing explanations for simple patterns in recorded measurements is a Level 3 activity. Beginning to relate their conclusions to patterns in data is a Level 4 activity.)

Sheet 2★★ asks the children to gather information, enter it on a simple 2-column table and to use this information to complete the pictogram. They then make a simple analysis using the data on the pictogram. (Using simple tables is a Level 2 activity, simple analysis of data is Level 3.)

Sheet 3★★ asks the children to record their observations using a simple 2-column table which has been prepared for them. (Level 2) They then complete the prepared bar chart and answer questions from it. After that they draw a conclusion, with help if needed. (Level 3)

Sheet 4★★★ Here, the children design their own table and bar chart. They draw a conclusion from the data and consider the evidence. (Relating conclusions to patterns in data is a Level 4 activity.)

Sheet 5 is a record of an individual child's achievements for them to complete in language they might use.

Background information

Turning ideas into a form that can be investigated

Ideas such as 'My cat likes/does not like chicken' can lead other children into saying what their cats eat.

Ask the children to pose questions about each other's cats: 'What does your cat eat?' 'Does she eat fish?' 'Who else's cat eats fish?' 'What else do cats eat?'

Then encourage them to make a general question:

- 'Do all cats like chicken/fish/lamb/beef?' and develop this into a general question that can form the basis of a worthwhile test:
- Which foods do our cats eat?

This will provide evidence that can be analysed in several ways and lead to discussion about how useful the evidence is as the basis for a conclusion.

Deciding how many animals should be investigated and the range of foods to be considered

The larger the sample the better, so encourage the children to think about all the cats they know or know about and how to find out what they eat. When discussing the range of food to be surveyed, the children will be able to list a variety from their own experience. This is a good opportunity to use the children's ideas, develop them into a practical test and base this on the children's decisions.

Presenting evidence in a suitable bar chart or pictogram

The tables on the Sheets 1 to 4 help the children to organise their information and to compile a chart from the table. A class bar chart with a larger sample will enable the children to see the same process and reinforce the learning.

Deciding whether the evidence is sufficient to draw conclusions

The evidence is sufficient to draw conclusions such as: 'The cats we know eat these foods.' 'Most of these cats eat x, about half eat y and very few eat z.' But the children will see the limitations such as: 'We don't know if this is the same for all the cats in our village/town/country.'

The evidence will always be improved by taking a larger and more diverse sample. There are other questions which arise from the evidence:

- Why do so few cats eat...? (Perhaps they are not given it.)
- Can we really tell which is a cat's favourite food?

Name .... Date ....

What do animals eat?

Some children made a list of birds they saw and found out what they eat. They found out about fourteen kinds of bird.

This bar chart shows how many kinds of bird eat each sort of food.

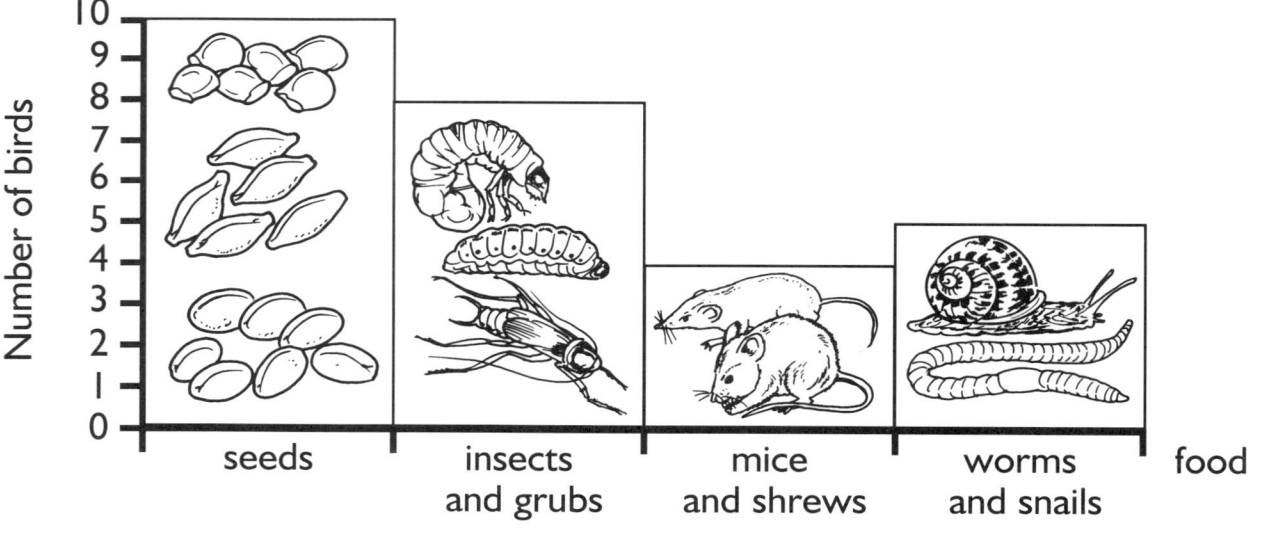

Looking at the results of the survey:

How many kinds of bird eat insects and grubs? ....

How many kinds of bird eat mice and shrews? ....

Which food is eaten by most birds? ....

Which food is eaten by fewest birds? ....

Why does the total add up to more than fourteen?

....

Which of these conclusions can you draw from this bar chart?

❏ All birds eat seeds.

❏ Most birds eat seeds.

❏ More birds in our survey eat seeds than other foods.

Name .... Date ....

What do our pets eat?

Tick which food the cats eat. Add any other food they eat.	
Chicken	
Fish	
Rabbit	

You can:

a) record your results on a bar chart
   OR

b) use the cats at the bottom of the sheet to make a pictogram.

How many cats eat chicken? ....

How many cats eat rabbit? ....

Which food do most of these cats eat? ....

Cut out these cats for the pictogram.

Name .... Date ....

What do our pets eat?

Tick which food the cats eat. Add any other food they eat.	
Chicken	
Fish	
Rabbit	

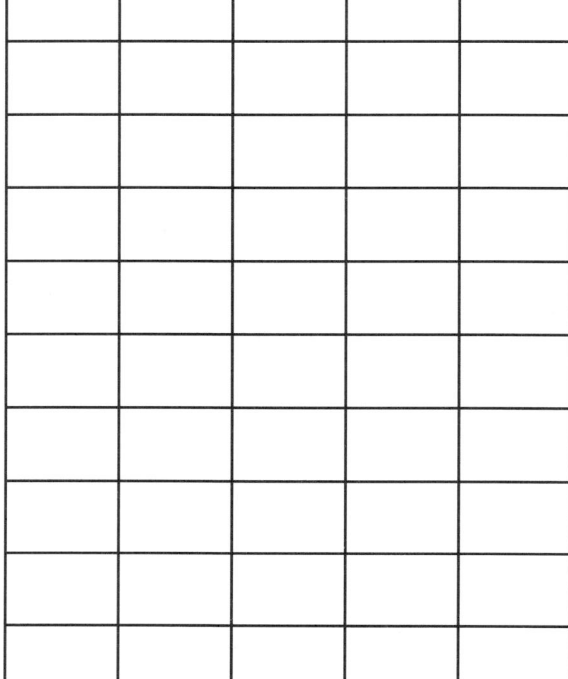

Number of cats

Foods

How many cats eat chicken? ....

How many cats eat rabbit? ....

Which food do most cats eat? ....

Which food do fewest cats eat? ....

What conclusion can you draw from this bar chart?

....

....

Name .... Date ....

What do our pets eat?

Use this table:

Use the results from your group to make a bar chart showing how many cats eat each kind of food.

Draw your bar chart on a piece of squared paper.

Which food do most cats eat? ....

Which food do fewest cats eat? ....

What is your conclusion? ....

....

Is it what you predicted? ....

Look at the bar chart of the results for the whole class. Are the results different? Say why this is.

....

....

Can you say which is the cats' favourite food? ....

Explain your answer. ....

....

How could we get better evidence for what cats eat? ....

....

Name .... Date ....

What do our pets eat?

Raising questions

☐ I can ask questions about what our pets eat.

☐ I can suggest a question which can be tested.

Suggesting how to find the answer to a question

☐ I can decide how many animals to investigate.

☐ I can suggest the range of foods to consider.

Making pictograms and bar charts

☐ I can fill in a table and a pictogram and talk about it. (Level 3)

☐ I can fill in a table and a bar chart and answer questions about it. (Level 3)

☐ I can design my own table and bar chart and analyse the results. (Level 4)

Characteristics of materials:
Which paper absorbs water best?

Learning objectives

Children should learn:

- to **plan a test** to compare the absorbency of different papers, deciding what evidence to collect, considering what to change, what to keep the same and what to measure
- to **make comparisons** and **draw conclusions**.

Lesson notes

 Approximate timing: 1.5 hours

Type of scientific enquiry

This Sc1 enquiry will give children the opportunity to tackle a whole investigation based on fair testing.

Introduction

Ask the children if they have seen advertisements on TV for kitchen rolls. It is a good idea to record one of these adverts on video to show the children to stimulate discussion at the start of this investigation. Show the children a couple of examples of absorbent paper. You can ask questions such as:

- What type of claims do advertisers make about paper towels?
- What makes a good paper towel? (Introduce the words 'absorb' and 'absorbent' here).

- How could we test which type of paper is best at absorbing water?

At this point children will put forward their suggestions. At first these tend to concentrate on the use of paper towels to mop up spills. Ask the children to evaluate the effectiveness of suggestions.

- How easy will it be to put the papers into order doing it that way?
- Is there a way that we can **measure** how much water each type of paper absorbs?

Some of the suggestions you are likely to get include:

- dip the paper in a known volume of water; measure how much water has gone when we remove the paper
- pour a known volume of water through the paper (perhaps in a funnel); measure how much water comes through
- dip the end of the paper in a little water; measure how far up the water rises in a set time.

Concentrate on aspects of fair testing:

- What are we changing?
- What are we measuring to see which paper is best?
- What are we keeping the same?

Sheets 1, 2 and 3 offer differentiated support in this planning phase of the investigation.

If time permits, close observation of the different papers to be tested using a hand lens or microscope can provide the basis for making predictions at this point.

Group work

Depending on the resources available, groups might be able to try out their suggestions from the introduction. On the other hand, you might decide as a whole class which is the best method to use and then all groups use this method.

Sheet 4 will help those who need support recording the results of their tests.

Whole class

This concluding session should focus on the comparison of results to produce a sequence of absorbency. The children can do this on the basis of visual comparison, but some type of measurement will tell us the relative differences between each type of paper. Sheet 4 has the results table followed by the sequencing activity.

Differentiated Sc1 learning outcomes

Planning

- with help, decides what to change, what to measure and what to keep the same
- decides what to change, what to measure and what to keep the same.

Concluding

- with help, uses visual comparisons to sequence the results of their tests
- uses visual comparisons to sequence the results of their tests
- uses measurements to sequence the results of their tests
- uses measurements to sequence the results of their tests and explains why their results are consistent with the order of absorbency they suggest.

Using the differentiated sheets

Sheets 1★, 2★★, and 3★★★ These sheets support children in planning a fair test with increasing decision making required progressing from Sheet 1 to Sheet 3. (Varying one factor whilst keeping others the same is a Level 4 skill.)

Sheet 4★★ This sheet is a recording sheet for those who benefit from the use of a writing frame to present their results and conclusion. (The use of the table and concluding correctly provide evidence for Level 3 skills.)

Sheet 5★★ This sheet is a Skill Sheet which requires children to read volumes of water, fill in a table, draw a bar chart and sequence the results. (Levels 3 and 4)

Sheet 6 This is the pupil record sheet to complete for this enquiry. Some children will need help filling this in.

Background information

Planning

This investigation provides an excellent opportunity to teach the skills of fair testing. Many children will recognise the need for fair testing when we are comparing the properties of different things and will suggest factors to control. Help may be needed by demonstrating an 'unfair test' to start with.

A variety of methods can be tried here illustrating the creative nature of science. Children will be very well motivated if they are given the chance to use a method that they suggested themselves.

Concluding

Children will have results to compare the absorbency of each paper. Although visual comparisons will answer the original question, they do not give us accurate information about the relative differences between the papers. Stressing the useful information we get from measurements will encourage children to build measurement into the planning of future investigations.

Having tried a variety of methods in the lesson, you can also have more faith in your conclusions if there is consistency between the order of absorbency across methods.

Absorbency

Paper is made from wood pulp. The fibres of cellulose are rearranged in the process of milling to produce various grades of paper. Papers are categorised by their weight (per ream/500 sheets) with lighter papers having more space between fibres and thinner sheets generally being more absorbent. These can draw up the water between fibres.

Name .... Date ....

Which paper absorbs water best?

Plan

We will find out which type of paper absorbs best by

....

....

....

Tick the correct box below:

We will change:
- ❑ The size of the paper
- ❑ The volume of water used
- ❑ The type of paper
- ❑ The time we let the water soak in

We will measure: .... to judge which paper absorbs water best.

Tick the correct boxes below:

We will keep the same:

- ❑ The size of the paper
- ❑ The volume of water used
- ❑ The type of paper
- ❑ The time we let the water soak in

If there is anything else you need to keep the same in each test, write it here:

....

....

Name .... Date ....

Which paper absorbs water best?

In our test we plan to see how far water soaks up strips of each paper.

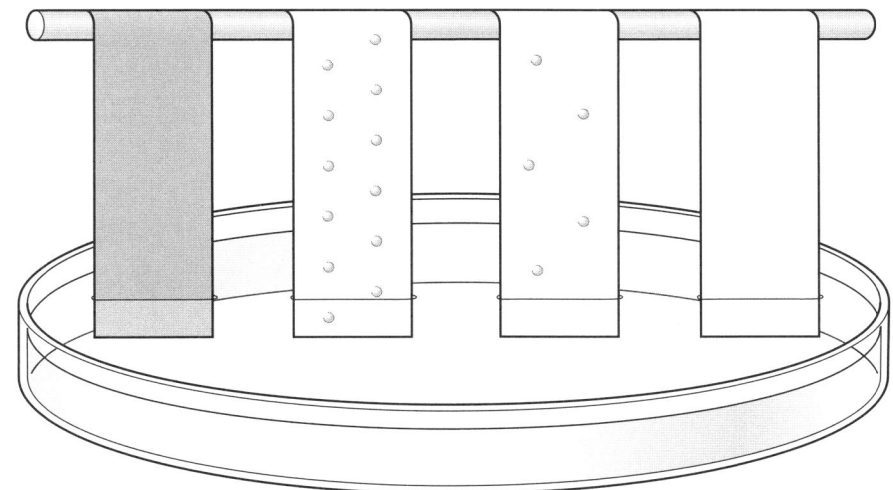

We will change: The type of paper

We will measure: ....

We will keep these things the same:

....

....

....

Name .... Date ....

Which paper absorbs water best?

Plan

We will find out which paper is best by ....

....

....

....

So we will change: ....

We will measure: ....

And we will keep these things the same: ....

....

....

Name .... Date ....

Which paper absorbs water best?

My results

What are you measuring to judge how much water gets absorbed?

Fill this in the top of the second column of the table below:

Type of paper tested	

My conclusion

From my results I can put the paper we tested into this order:

1. .... (most absorbent)

2. ....

3. ....

4. .... (least absorbent)

I decided on this order because ....

....

....

Name .... Date ....

Which paper absorbs water best?

A group poured the same volume of water through different paper towels. They measured how much water came through each paper towel. Here are the results of their test:

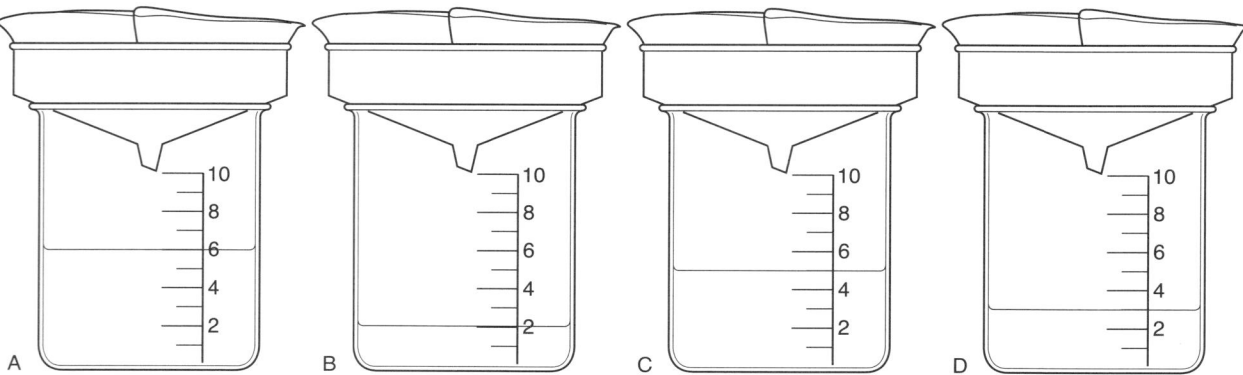

a) Put their results into the table below:

Paper towel	Volume of water that passed through (ml)
A	
B	
C	
D	

b) Draw a bar chart to show their results on a piece of squared paper.

c) Put the paper towels into order (with the most absorbent first):

1. .... (most absorbent) 2. ....

3. .... 4. ....

Name .... Date ....

Which paper absorbs water best?

Planning

❑ With help, I can plan what to change, what to measure and what to keep the same to carry out a fair test. (Level 3)

❑ I can plan what to change, what to measure and what to keep the same to carry out a fair test. (Level 4)

Concluding

❑ I can put the different types of paper into order based on how well they absorb water. (Level 2)

❑ I can put the different types of paper into order based on how well they absorb water, and explain how I decided on the order from my results. (Level 3)

Habitats: Do woodlice prefer damp conditions?

Nelson Thornes Ref: PS Kit 4.2.5

Learning objectives

Children should learn:

● to **pose questions** about organisms and the habitat in which they live and **make predictions**

● to **decide what evidence to collect and design a fair test**

● to **make reliable observations** of organisms

● to **indicate whether their prediction was valid and to explain findings in scientific terms**.

Lesson notes

⏱ Approximate timing: 2 hours with observations taking place over more than one school day.

Type of scientific enquiry

This scientific enquiry will give the children the opportunity to carry out a biological enquiry.

Introduction

Collect as many woodlice as possible. One practical way to do this is to go out early with a few children and collect the woodlice from under stones, wood, and vegetation. Ask the children to make notes on where they were found and what the conditions were.

Back in the classroom the children describe the habitat in which they found the woodlice to the rest of the class. Give all the children time to observe them carefully, to ask questions and to talk about their behaviour. (See notes on woodlice in Background Information on page 21.)

Now that they know something about the organisms, ask the children to pose questions about their habitat and the conditions there. It was probably dark and damp, so encourage them to ask if that is what woodlice 'like'. Introduce 'prefer'.

● Which conditions do woodlice prefer? Make predictions.

● Do they really prefer to be in the dark?

● How do we know that they prefer damp conditions?

● How can we find out?

Discuss plans for a fair test, take the children's suggestions, develop them, and help them to make the decisions:

● What would be the evidence to answer our question/s?

● How can we give them a choice to see which they prefer?

● How many woodlice? How long shall we leave them?

● How will we collect the evidence?

One way is to prepare a 'choice chamber'; use a plastic box with a lid and a division down the middle with access to both sides.

- To test if they prefer damp conditions, line one half with damp kitchen paper and the other with dry paper, cover with a clear material that lets air in. (They can't climb a smooth surface, so they shouldn't get out.) You might put the box into a dark place.

- To test if they prefer dark conditions use another box and cover one half to exclude as much light as possible, cover the other half with clear material, put the woodlice in the light end and shine a light onto them.

- To test if they prefer both damp and dark, a third box could be organised with three choices — dark and dry, light and damp, and dark and damp.

Do several tests to provide more evidence.

Individual and group work

The children set up the investigation, planning as they go using Sheets 2, 3 and/or 4. Ask the children questions to find out their understanding of a 'fair' test and their planning skills. Discuss their observations, any problems and any adjustments to the test that they have made or ought to make.

Whole class

Discuss the findings, ask individuals and groups to describe how they did their test and what results they have. Discuss the results and any problems — the results may not be clear-cut, some groups may have slightly different results. Suggest putting the results together to see if the result is clearer. Talk about how reliable the evidence is.

Draw conclusions — What have we found out? What can we say about the conditions these woodlice prefer? Is the evidence good enough to say this? Was our sample of woodlice large enough?

- Match the conclusions to the children's predictions.

- Ask for explanations in scientific terms — most of the woodlice in our test preferred the damp kitchen paper to the dry paper. We found them in damp conditions in their habitat. So we think that woodlice prefer damp conditions.

Differentiated Sc1 learning outcomes

Posing questions about organisms and their habitat; making predictions

- makes predictions based on practical evidence — Woodlice are found in damp conditions, so I predict that they like the damp.

- poses a question based on their prediction — Do woodlice really like damp conditions best? Do woodlice prefer dark to light conditions? Do woodlice prefer dark and damp conditions?

Planning – deciding on what evidence to collect

- recognises what evidence would answer the question

- suggests what evidence would answer the question

- suggests that the woodlice would need to make a choice in the test.

Designing a fair test

- suggests that they should conduct a fair test

- shows that they can vary one factor and keep others the same.

Observing

- uses appropriate senses to observe the behaviour of the woodlice

- makes relevant and reliable observations.

Drawing conclusions

- describes their observations — most of the woodlice went onto the damp paper

- draws a conclusion from their observations and evidence — so woodlice must like (prefer) damp places

- draws a conclusion from the whole class evidence, knowing this makes it more reliable

- matches their prediction to their conclusion

- if necessary, changes their mind in the face of the evidence.

Explaining their findings

- provides an explanation for their result — the woodlice like it in a damp place

● provides an explanation in scientific terms — woodlice prefer damp conditions because...

Using the differentiated sheets

Sheet 1★★★ helps the children understand a fair test, and gives them practice in planning a fair test.

Sheet 2★★ asks the children to carry out a fair test with some help, make careful observations, record their results and draw a conclusion from the evidence, matching it to their prediction. (Level 3)

Sheet 3★★★ asks the children to plan and carry out a fair test, with help if necessary. (Level 3/4)

Sheet 4★★★ asks the children to plan and carry out a whole investigation and explain the results in scientific terms. (These are Level 4 activities.)

Sheet 5 is a record for an individual child to complete, with help if necessary.

Background information

Posing questions about organisms and the habitat in which they live and making predictions

Small organisms such as woodlice, snails and worms provide children with a great opportunity to ask questions —

● What is it? Where does it live?
● What does it eat? How many legs has it got?
● Can woodlice see?

Encourage them to pose questions during the initial observation of the animals.

The teacher can ask questions which steer the children into thinking about questions which could lead to a test:

● Do they like damp places?
● Do they live there because it's dark?
● Is this where their food is?
● Do they feel safe there?

Then onto:
● How do we know that...? How could we find out?

Predictions come before, between and at the end of posing questions.

Most predictions will come from what the children observe, hear about and, perhaps, know already – 'If they live in damp places, they must like them.' 'I think they prefer dark places.' 'I think they prefer both dark and damp places.'

Planning – deciding what evidence to collect and designing a fair test

Through discussion, questions and suggestions from the children and the teacher, the children will be able to make decisions about the evidence which will help them answer their question. They will probably need some help over deciding that the woodlice need to be offered a choice and about deciding on the number of woodlice to use.

Much scientific enquiry involves testing to find out whether a prediction is correct or not. This activity involves a fair test to check a prediction.

One factor under scrutiny is dampness, so this is what is changed to give the woodlice a choice — dampness or dryness. As far as possible, other conditions should stay the same, for example, temperature, light, area, substrate (paper).

At this stage, children plan a test 'on the hoof'; they think out what to do in the course of doing it, they do not anticipate what will happen in unfamiliar situations such as this one. It can help to make some of the decisions for them — you're going to use this box and kitchen paper. The next steps then become simpler:

● How can we give the woodlice a choice?
● Might the woodlice want to get away?
● How can we stop them?

Most of the children will know if a test is unfair — if we put some woodlice in the dark and damp and some in the dry and light, for example. They are beginning to learn that a fair test involves changing one thing only. They are at the beginning of knowing about changing one factor while keeping others the same. When carrying out their test, they may spot unfairness whilst doing the test and change the test for themselves.

The tables on the Sheets are also designed to help the children with this process of planning and conducting their tests.

Making reliable observations of organisms

The more times a scientific test is done, and the more people who conduct the test, the more reliable is the evidence for a conclusion. Also, it must be carried out systematically and carefully. Observations are, therefore, more reliable if they are repeated, confirmed by others in the group and supported by other groups doing a similar test. In biological enquiries, the larger the sample size, the more faith we can have in our results.

Indicating whether their prediction was valid and explaining findings in scientific terms

If the evidence supports a prediction, it is a valid one — 'I was right!' Predictions don't always come at the same stage in an investigation; children may make a prediction, offering an answer to a question, right at the beginning of an investigation, or after having explored or considered other information during their enquiry.

The scientific terms the children might use in a scientific explanation might be habitat, condition, woodlice, organism and prefer — plus a reason:

'Woodlice prefer to live in a habitat where the conditions are damp. We think this because we found them in a damp place and they moved to a damp place in our test.'

Woodlice

We all live close to at least two species of woodlice. The most common woodlice around homes and gardens are the Common Shiny Woodlouse (Oniscus Asellus), Common Rough Woodlouse (Porcellio Scaber) and the Common Pill Bug (Armadillidium vulgare) — which rolls up instead of running away. Around 37 species are known to be breeding in a variety of habitats outdoors.

Their closest relatives are crabs, lobsters and daphnia (water fleas). They belong to the order Isopoda and the class Crustacea. They have evolved from ancestors that lived on the sea bed. They are decomposers, which means they chew dead wood and plants, and their faecal pellets decompose rapidly to add essential nutrients to the earth. They are not destructive pests, but an important part of our environment.

Woodlice have many natural predators: common shrews, hedgehogs, frogs, newts and lizards; little owls and foxes; spiders, centipedes, harvestmen and beetles.

They are segmented animals with a rigid exoskeleton and jointed limbs. Their eyes can be compound or simple. They use their antennae as sense organs. Their mouths are under the head. They are born with six pairs of legs and a seventh pair appears after the first moult. They are very vulnerable to predators whilst they are moulting as their body is very soft underneath the exoskeleton. The young are born alive and are white; they spend the early part of their life in a brood pouch on the female's underside.

Their normal reaction to predators is to run away or roll into a ball. Their reaction to light is to hide in a dark place; and they move towards dampness. They need damp conditions to maintain their body equilibrium and take in water by drinking, in their food, or by sucking it into their bodies. They also absorb water through the cuticle.

They come out of their place of hiding to feed. They are basically plant eaters; they occasionally eat flesh if they come across dead or decaying animals, including other woodlice that are dying or moulting.

Woodlice are easy to keep in school. They can be kept in small containers such as lunch boxes for short periods, and in large containers such as a fish tank for longer periods. Put about 10cm of old compost in the bottom, add woodland leaf litter next as a source of food, and put pieces of bark, wood, slate and stones on top. They like clay flower pots, cardboard tubes, fir cones and shells as places to live in. They can be fed on all sorts of foods — carrots, potatoes, parsnips and mushrooms, for example. Keep the contents of the tank moist but not wet, by spraying regularly.

(Adapted from: www.dryad.demon.co.uk/julies/woodlice.htm)

Name .... Date ....

Planning a test

1. You want to find out whether woodlice prefer **damp** places.

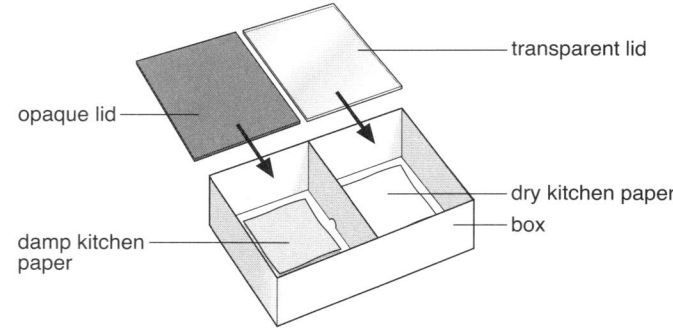

opaque lid

transparent lid

damp kitchen paper

dry kitchen paper

box

Say why this test is **not** a fair test ....

....

....

....

2. In your test to see whether they prefer damp places

What will you change? ....

What will you observe? ....

What will you keep the same? ....

....

....

3. How many woodlice will you use? ....

Why? ....

....

Name .... Date ....

Do woodlice prefer damp places to dry places?

In the first box draw the woodlice where they were when you first put them in.

In the second box draw them where they were after some time had passed.

You are looking at them from above.

Damp
Dry

Damp
Dry

What happened?

....

This is how we made a fair test:

This is what we changed	This is what we kept the same	This is what we observed
the water		

What did the woodlice do after they were put into the box?

....

What is your conclusion? ....

Was your prediction correct?...

Write what you noticed and found out about woodlice ....

....

....

....

© Lawrie Ryan and Rosemary Sherrington, Nelson Thornes Ltd, 2002

Name .... Date ....

How do we know that woodlice prefer darkness?

Our prediction ....

Our plans

We will put some woodlice .... and shine a light on them.

We will use ....

We will make the test fair like this:

We will change ....

We will observe ....

We will keep these the same ....

This is what happened ....

Our conclusion is ....

Our evidence is ....

Our prediction was right/wrong, probably right/probably wrong. (Underline the correct answer.)

Draw a woodlouse and write what you have observed and found out about them.

Name .... Date ....

Do woodlice prefer dark and damp conditions?

What is your prediction? ....
....

Plan a fair test

This is what we will change	This is what we will observe	This is what we will keep the same

What do you expect to happen? ....
....

What did happen? ....
....

What is your conclusion about what woodlice prefer? ....
....

What is your evidence? ....
What other test evidence is there to support yours?
....

Say why you think woodlice prefer these conditions
....

Draw a woodlouse here.   ....

Identify which species it is: ....

                                         ....

Name .... Date ....

What conditions do woodlice prefer?

Posing questions

☐ I can make predictions about where woodlice like to live. (Level 4)

☐ I can pose a question based on my prediction.

Deciding what evidence to collect

☐ I agreed that woodlice will go into damp places if they like them.

☐ I suggested that woodlice will go into damp (dark) places as they prefer them. (Level 4)

☐ I suggested that woodlice should be able to choose whether they go into dark and damp places.

Designing a fair test

☐ I know that we must do a fair test. (Level 3)

☐ I know how to change one thing and keep others the same. (Level 4)

Name .... Date ....

What conditions do woodlice prefer?

Observing

☐ I watched carefully to see what the woodlice did.

☐ I observed carefully over time and looked at others' results to check my own. (Level 4)

Drawing conclusions

☐ I can draw a conclusion from my observations and match it to my prediction. (Level 2)

☐ I know that using evidence from the whole class makes it more reliable and I know when my prediction is valid.

☐ I think that woodlice like damp places because my test showed this. (Level 3)

☐ I can explain that woodlice prefer certain conditions because of the type of habitat they live in. (Level 4/5)

Keeping warm: Which is the best thermal insulator?

Nelson Thornes Ref: PS Kit 4.3.3

Learning objectives

Children should learn:

- to **turn an idea** about how to keep things warm **into a form that can be investigated**

- to **plan a fair test** deciding what to change, what to keep the same and what to measure

- to **make careful measurements** of temperature at regular time intervals

- to **record results in a table** and to use these to **draw conclusions**

- that some materials are good thermal insulators.

Lesson notes

 Approximate timing: 2 hours

Type of scientific enquiry

This Sc1 enquiry will give children the opportunity to tackle a whole investigation based on fair testing.

Introduction

Set the context of the investigation in a real life situation. For example, you might ask how we insulate a hot water tank at home or how we can keep a hot drink warm.

- How can we check how hot the water/drink is as time passes?

Introduce the term 'thermal insulation' and show the class the materials you are about to test. Give the children a chance to pose their own questions and to decide what to change, what to keep the same and what to measure.

- What question shall we investigate?

- How can we carry out a fair test?

Support should be offered where necessary. (Sheet 1 is available for this purpose.)

Group work

The availability of resources will determine the approach adopted. If materials are limited, you could agree that all groups carry out the test in the same way, for example, taking the temperature of the water every 2 minutes for 20 minutes. Each group can then test one particular material. If you use a common method, the data can be drawn together for a whole class discussion of results.

The class should be familiar with using thermometers before this investigation (some practice is provided on Sheet 4). Some children will be able to plan their own table to record their results, but others will need support (Sheets 2 and 3). The higher attaining children will be starting to display their results on a line graph, again with support offered as necessary (Sheet 3).

Whole class

The discussion of the evidence from graphs is important in this investigation. If you have a couple of temperature sensors available in school, you can show the lines for two materials 'unfolding before the children's eyes' on a computer screen. Alternatively choose a couple of sets of results to compare:

- Which is cooling down faster?
- How can you tell?
- Which material is the better thermal insulator?
- Can you put all the materials tested in order?
- Why do you think that some materials are good thermal insulators?

Differentiated Sc1 learning outcomes

Questioning

- with help, turns an idea about how to keep things warm into a form that can be investigated
- turns an idea about how to keep things warm into a form that can be investigated.

Planning

- with help, decides what to change, what to measure and what to keep the same given guidance on a writing frame
- plans a fair test, deciding what to change, what to measure and what to keep the same.

Measuring

- with help, measures temperatures at regular time intervals
- measures temperatures accurately at regular time intervals.

Recording

- given a table, fills in times and temperatures
- designs own table and fills in times and temperatures.

Concluding

- with help, compares the thermal insulation properties of different materials and puts them in order

- compares the thermal insulation properties of different materials and puts them in order, explaining why their results are consistent with the sequence they suggest.

Using the differentiated sheets

Sheet 1★ This sheet is aimed at supporting those children who need lots of support planning their own fair test. Help can be given if necessary to identify which factors to keep the same in each test.

Sheet 2★ This sheet provides the tables for groups to fill in for each material they test. (The use of a simple table is a Level 2 skill.)

Sheet 3★★ This sheet helps children record their results in one table, draw a graph and make conclusions. (Children using this sheet will be displaying skills from Levels 3 to 5, depending on the support given.)

Sheet 4★★★ This Skill Sheet requires children to read scales, fill in a table and draw a line graph (Level 4/5).

Sheet 5 This is the pupil record sheet to complete for this enquiry. Some children will need help filling this in.

Background information

Turning an idea into a form that can be investigated

Talking about keeping food warm and cold will stimulate children to suggest factors that make some materials good insulators and the ways we can make them as effective as possible. They should be encouraged to frame their own questions to which it is possible to find the answer by carying out an investigation.

Planning

Finding the best thermal insulator is difficult to set up as a truly fair test. Controlling the thickness of materials is hard to achieve, but this will be discussed in the evaluation at the end of the investigation. The range of time over which we take our measurements is also tricky to plan without a trial run or guidance from the teacher.

Measuring

There are two types of measurement that we can take to answer our question. The less demanding way is to take an initial temperature then a final temperature after a set time. However, the learning objective requires the reading of temperatures at regular time intervals. This gives us more information about the rate of cooling. (Is it steady? Does it fall quicker at first?)

Concluding

Most children will be able to sequence their thermal insulators from the results obtained. Higher attaining children can be supported to record their results on a graph and then talk in more detail about the temperature changes they recorded. As mentioned in the lesson notes, the use of data logging to produce the graphs will free children to think about their conclusions more deeply.

Thermal insulation

Heat energy is transferred from warmer to colder places. Thermal insulators make this transfer more difficult. They reduce the rate of transfer from the surroundings to an ice cube, or the rate of transfer from a hot drink to the surroundings.

Gases are good thermal insulators and most insulation is made of materials that have a gas trapped inside. For example, expanded polystyrene and foams have carbon dioxide gas blown into the plastic as it sets.

Name .... Date ....

Which is the best thermal insulator?

In our tests we plan to measure which material is best at keeping water hot.

We will change: | The type of material |

We will measure: | The temperature every 5 minutes for each material |

We will keep these things the same: ....

....

....

....

Name .... Date ....

Which is the best thermal insulator?

My results for ....

Time (minutes)	Temperature (°C)
0	

My results for ....

Time (minutes)	Temperature (°C)
0	

My results for ....

Time (minutes)	Temperature (°C)
0	

Name .... Date ....

Which is the best thermal insulator?

My results

Time (mins)	Temperature (°C)			
	Material	Material	Material	Material ....
0				

Now show all your results on the same graph on a piece of graph paper.

My conclusion

From my results I can put the materials we tested into this order:

1. .... (best thermal insulator)

2. ....

3. ....

4. .... (worst thermal insulator)

I decided on this order because

....

....

Name .... Date ....

Water cooling down

A group looked at the temperature of hot water as it cooled down.

Their results are shown below:

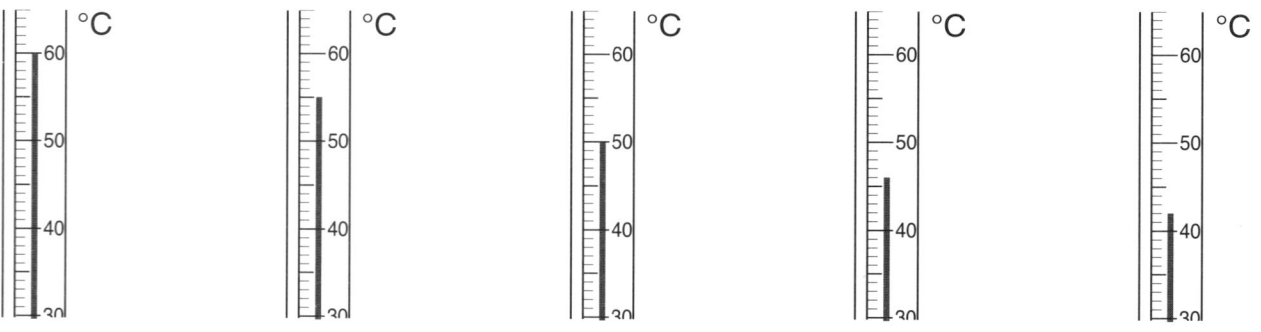

Put these results into the table below:

Time (min)	Temperature (°C)

Now show the results on a graph below:

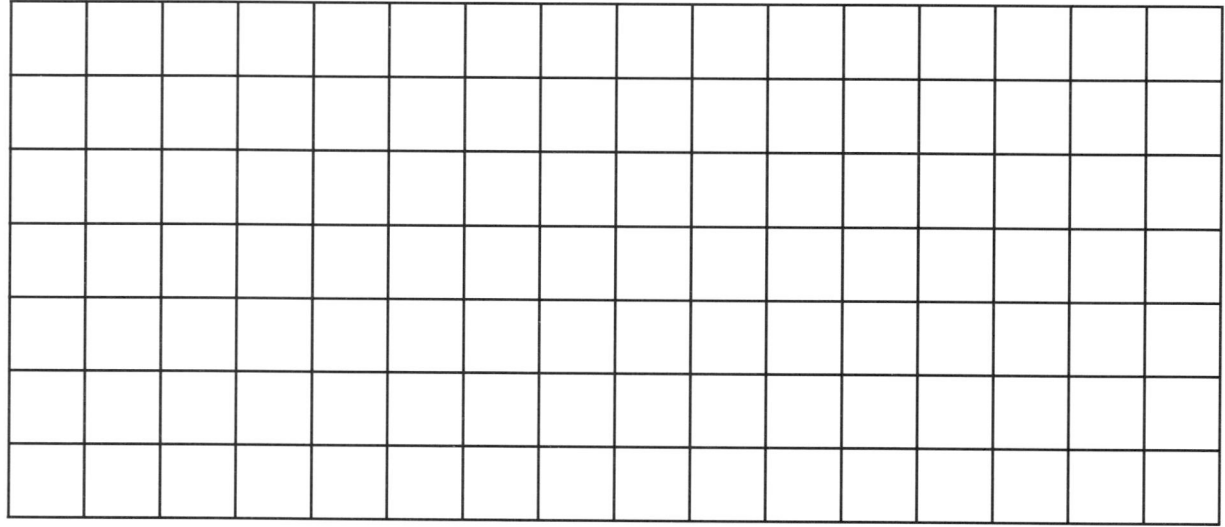

Name .... Date ....

Which is the best thermal insulator?

Planning

☐ With help, I can plan what to change, what to measure and what to keep the same to carry out a fair test. (Level 3)

☐ I can plan what to change, what to measure and what to keep the same to carry out a fair test. (Level 4)

Measuring

☐ I can measure temperature using a thermometer. (Level 3)

☐ I can measure how the temperature of hot water changes with time. (Level 4)

☐ I can take accurate measurements of the temperature of hot water as it changes with time. (Level 5)

Recording

☐ I can record a series of measurements in a table and draw a graph showing the results for one material. (Level 4)

☐ I can show all my results on one graph to help me compare each material. (Level 5)

Friction: Investigating parachutes

Nelson Thornes Ref: PS Kit 4.5.6

Learning objectives

Children should learn:

● to **plan a fair test** saying **what they will change, what they will keep the same and what they will measure**

● to **make measurements of time**

● to **identify a pattern in the results** and to **explain it in terms of air resistance**.

Lesson notes

⏱ Approximate timing: 2 hours. Extra time is needed for the children to practise with the parachutes.

Prepare parachutes of, for example, black bin liner with plastic of various sized squares and a variety of small objects of different weights: small weights, balls of modelling clay, metal washers, etc. The modelling clay is easiest to attach to the parachute strings.

Type of scientific enquiry

This scientific enquiry gives the children the opportunity to plan and carry out a fair test.

Introduction

Introduce the activity by asking the children to explore what happens when they drop a variety of small objects with and without parachutes. Ask them to observe carefully any differences they find in the way things fall through the air. Then call them all together to talk about what they have found out.

● What happened when you dropped the objects? — 'they fell', 'gravity,'…

● What happened when you dropped them with a parachute attached to them? — 'they fell', 'they fell slower only if the parachute opened'.

Find out if all the parachutes have the same effect — 'the bigger ones fell the slowest', 'the small ones fell faster than the big ones'.

● What happens when you change the weight of the object? — 'If you make it heavier, it falls faster with the same parachute', 'If you make it lighter, it falls more slowly'.

Elicit their ideas about how this happens: 'the parachute spreads out in the air', 'it holds the air in itself'.

● So what is the air doing? — 'it's holding the parachute up', 'stopping it falling down'.

Establish that this force is called air resistance and that the friction of the air slows things on the way down. Talk this through carefully with the children, encourage them to think about and discuss their ideas of what is happening.

Now that we think we know what happens when things fall with parachutes, what questions could we ask that might make a good investigation?

● Does a large parachute fall faster than a small one with the same weight attached?

Talk about parachutes with holes in them.

● Does a parachute with holes in fall more slowly than one with no holes in?

Help the children to make plans.

● What will you do? — Let them practise first and make predictions. Drop them down a stairwell, or use fairy cake cases of different sizes or with/without holes. Test two different parachutes with the same weight attached. Use two parachutes the same size, one with holes. Use two parachutes of different sizes.

● What will you measure? — which one reaches the floor first. The time it takes to reach the floor. Use a clock or stopwatch.

● How will you make the test a fair one? Drop two together, see which reaches the floor first. Drop one at a time from the same height, timing them. Do the test several times.

Individual and group work

The children plan and carry out their tests, using Sheets 2, 3 and 4 and complete sections 1 to 4. As they work, discuss with them their ideas about the science skills needed — what to change, keep the same and measure, and making careful measurements of time. Encourage them to be critical of the way they carry out their tests and to improve them as they go.

Whole class

Discuss their results, their accuracy, and problems and any other points which arose from the investigation, particularly the measurement of time and achieving accuracy.

● What patterns can you see in your results?

The bigger parachute took longer to fall than the small one. It took .... seconds more than the small one.

● Can you explain how a big parachute (or one with no holes in) falls more slowly?

i.e. 'because it trapped more air', 'the air stopped it falling', 'it's the air resistance', 'the parachute with no holes in trapped more air — it fell slowly because the air stopped it falling quickly'.

Ask the children to complete their sheets.

Differentiated Sc1 learning outcomes

Planning and carrying out a fair test

● plans a fair test and, with help, says what they will change, keep the same and measure; with help, carries out a fair test

● plans a fair test saying what they will change, some factors they will keep the same and what they will measure; successfully varies one factor and keeps the others the same

● plans a fair test saying what they will change, the important factors they should not change and what they will measure; successfully carrying it out.

Making measurements of time

● measures with reasonable accuracy using a timer with a second hand

● selects suitable equipment

● measures carefully with a stop-clock

● measures carefully with a simple stop-watch

● repeats the measurements to get a more reliable measurement

● offers simple explanations for any differences in the repeated measurements.

Identifying a pattern in the results

● uses the results to show differences in the times

● compares the differences to indicate which was the slowest to fall

● suggests that the bigger the parachute, the slower it will fall.

Explaining the pattern

- makes a statement — the air is holding it up longer
- links cause and effect — it falls more slowly because of air resistance
- makes a generalisation — the larger the parachute, the more air resistance, so the slower it will fall.

Using the differentiated sheets

Sheet 1★ gives the children the opportunity to practise timing using three different timers.

Sheet 2★★ asks the children to plan and carry out a fair test with help, record their observations and explain a simple pattern in the results. They begin to be able to explain air resistance in terms of its effect on the parachutes. (Level 3)

Sheet 3★★★ asks the children to use tables to show that they can describe how to do a fair test, varying one factor while controlling others. They should indicate and explain patterns in the results, come to a conclusion and, with help if necessary, explain air resistance in terms of its effect on parachutes. (Level 4)

Sheet 4★★★ asks the children to write more extensively about their investigation, to plan a fair test, construct a table for the results, see patterns in the results, draw a valid conclusion from the evidence and explain their conclusion in terms of air resistance. Some children may be encouraged to generalise from the conclusion. (Level 4)

Sheet 5 – This is the pupil record sheet to complete for this enquiry.

Background information

Planning and carrying out fair tests

These science skills are often separated, but with children, they often occur together, as in this investigation. It is not until the children have explored the ways parachutes fall that they can begin to ask questions and consider the factors which they might change, keep the same and measure. As they find out what the parachutes do, they begin to make predictions, but to test their prediction, they need to set up a test where only one thing is changed and other things which might affect the movement of the parachute are kept the same. In this case, they measure the time various parachutes take to fall — working with an appropriate degree of accuracy. The children will continue to practise — for example, their techniques for dropping the parachutes until they are happy they have controlled this factor.

Making measurements of time

A number of children will have stop-watches and be able to use them with some accuracy, others will need to learn this skill. The easiest timer for children to use is a stop-clock with minutes and seconds. The classroom clock with a second hand is useful for this type of measurement, but requires the children to work out the time from where the second hand starts to where it stops.

Identifying a pattern in the results and explaining it

Pattern-seeking is a skill which involves seeing how observations are related to each other, in this case, the biggest parachute (or the one with no holes) is related to the slowest time falling.

Explaining a pattern of events is an important part of scientific activity. In this case, the reason is a fairly clear one, especially as the children have been learning about friction and water resistance and have been introduced to the idea of air resistance already. Some children will be able to generalise from this, linking cause and effect — The biggest parachute trapped the most air, which stopped it falling as quickly as the small one.

Air resistance

When objects move through air they experience the friction force of the air. This is called air resistance and acts in the opposite direction to the way the object is travelling. As an object falls through the air towards the ground, air resistance acts to slow its speed (velocity). Air resistance is acting against gravity. The air offers a greater resisting force to objects with a large surface area — such as a parachute.

Gravity is a term many children are aware of; if appropriate, talk about the force opposing air resistance as 'gravitational attraction' (which wins in the end).

Name .... Date ....

Investigating parachutes

Measuring time

Some children were dropping parachutes and measuring how long each one took to fall to the ground. Each group used a different timer. (Think about which timer you would use and explain why.)

Write the time it takes each parachute to fall.

Group 1 used a stop clock

Parachute 1 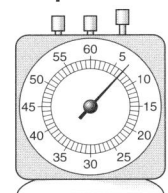 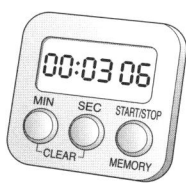 Parachute 2

....

Group 2 used a stop watch

Parachute 1  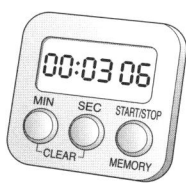 Parachute 2

....

Group 3 used the classroom clock

  Parachute 1

....

 Parachute 2

....

Name .... Date ....

Investigating parachutes

1. Our question is ....

2. This is how we plan to do a fair test

    We will change ....

    We will use a .... to time ....

    We will do each measurement .... times.

    We will not change ....

    ....

3. These are our results

Parachute	Time it took to fall to the floor (seconds)		
	First time	Second time	Third time
1			
2			
Difference in time			

4. What we noticed about the parachutes ....

   ....

5. We think this happened because ....

   ....

   ....

Name .... Date ....

Investigating parachutes

1. Our question ....

2. Our fair test

This is what we will change	This is what we will measure	This is what we will keep the same

3. Our results

Parachute	Time it took to fall to the floor (seconds)		
	First time	Second time	Third time
1			
2			
Difference in time			

4. What we noticed ....

....

5. Our conclusion ....

6. We think this is because ....

....

....

Name .... Date ....

Investigating air resistance

Use the headings to help you write about your investigation.

1. Question ....

....

2. Prediction ....

....

3. Plans for a fair test ....

....

....

4. Results

Parachute	Time it took to fall to the floor (seconds)		
	First time	Second time	Third time
1			
2			
Difference in time			

5. Patterns in the results ....

....

6. My explanation ....

....

....

7. Draw a picture of your parachute with arrows to show the direction of the forces acting on it. Use the back of this sheet.

Name .... Date ....

Friction: Investigating parachutes

Planning and carrying out a fair test

☐ I can plan a fair test with help. (Level 3)

☐ I did my test with some help keeping it fair. (Level 3)

☐ I know what to change, keep the same and measure in my test. (Level 4)

☐ I did my test in a fair way. (Level 4)

Making measurements of time

☐ I know what to use to time things.

☐ I can use a timer with a second hand and be accurate. (Level 4)

☐ I can use a stop watch correctly to measure seconds. (Level 5)

☐ I can use a clock and work out times in seconds. (Level 4)

☐ I know why I do a measurement more than once. (Level 4/5)

☐ I can suggest a reason why repeat measurements might be different. (Level 5)

Name .... Date ....

Friction: Investigating parachutes

Identifying a pattern in the results

❑ I can work out the differences in the times the parachutes took to fall. (Level 3)

❑ I saw that a big parachute falls slower than a small one. (Level 3)

❑ I suggested that the bigger the parachute, the slower it will fall. (Level 4)

Explaining the pattern

❑ I know that the air holds up a parachute and makes it fall slowly. (Level 3)

❑ I know that a parachute falls slowly because of air resistance. (Level 4)

❑ I said that the larger the parachute, the more air resistance there is, so the slower it will fall. (Level 5)

Keeping healthy: Investigating pulse rate

Nelson Thornes Ref: PS Kit 5.1.4

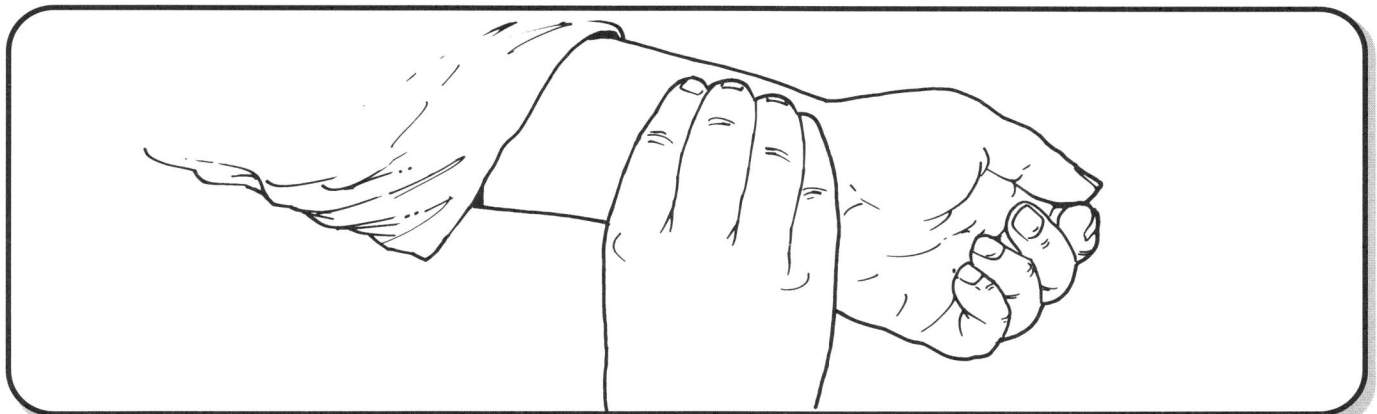

Learning objectives

Children should learn:

- to **identify factors** which could affect pulse rate and **make predictions** about the changes
- to **plan what evidence to collect** including the number of measurements of pulse rate to take and the number of children to use
- to **present results in a line graph and explain** what these show and whether they support the prediction.

Lesson notes

 Approximate timing 2 hours

Type of scientific enquiry

This scientific enquiry gives the children the opportunity to conduct an enquiry in a biological context in which sample size is important.

Introduction

Introduce the activity by sharing the objectives with the children, then showing them how to take their pulse rates. Ask them to take their pulse rate three times. Use several examples to show them how to work out an average.

Help the children to identify factors which might affect their pulse rates. Lead them through the process by asking questions. For example:

- What is your pulse rate?
  (These will vary between 80 and 90, although there may be exceptions.)
  What could affect it?

- Can you think what might make it go faster/slower?
  — breathing fast, running, sitting very still.
- Take running, how could we do an investigation to find out if we're right?
  — We could run about and take our pulse.

Help the children to be clear of the factors:

- What do you think of this idea? What factor are we changing? What factors must stay the same? What should we measure?

...and to plan as they try out the test:

- How many times should we do the test? What measurement should we take first?

Now ask for suggestions for the question to test
— How does exercise affect our pulse rate?
What do you predict will happen?
— Exercise will make our pulse rate increase.

Individual and group work

Ask the children to work on Sheet 2, 3 or 4 to plan their own investigation. One suggestion for a question which can be tested is:

How does running for 3 minutes (then resting for 3 minutes) affect my pulse rate?

Apart from the question, the children can take as many decisions about how to do their tests as possible.

Whole class

Discuss their planning at this stage. Discuss their predictions. Talk again about measuring pulse rate before and after and how many times to repeat their measurements.

Individual and group work

The children carry out their investigations. Check the children's ideas and understanding of factors and how they are manipulated, and the accuracy of their measurements.

Whole class

Discuss the tables of results. Introduce the idea of drawing line graphs from the data.

Use the headings from the tables — what we change (the activity) forms the horizontal axis and what we measure (pulse rate) forms the vertical axis.

Individual and group work

The children continue to use Sheets 2,3 and 4 with help, as necessary, from the teacher.

Whole class

Discuss the children's graphs and their explanations. Then ask a group of children to show their group graph. Ask about and compare individual and group graphs. What conclusions can you draw from each? Which might give better (more reliable) information? Show a large version of the line graph on Sheet 1 and discuss the validity of the conclusions which can be drawn from it. Ask the children to think carefully about their own conclusions, and, if necessary, rewrite them.

Differentiated Sc1 learning outcomes

Identifying factors and making predictions

- suggests that movement or exercise causes pulse to beat faster
- suggests that different forms of exercise increase the pulse at different rates
- suggests that exercising for longer increases pulse rate further
- suggests that pulse rate and heart rate are affected by exercise.

Planning what evidence to collect

- suggests taking the pulse after exercise
- suggests taking the pulse before and after and repeating the measurements
- suggests taking measurements of a number of children.

Presenting results on a line graph

- names the axes and plots the points on one person's graph, with help
- names the axes and plots the points, choosing the 'best'(mean, median or mode) number of several measurements
- constructs a line graph of the group's average pulse rates, choosing their own axes and plotting the points.

Interpreting their line graphs and whether they support the prediction

- says what the line graph shows and that it does or does not support their prediction
- includes the factors they considered
- draws a conclusion from the evidence on the line graph and compares it to their prediction
- describes some limitation of their work.

Using the differentiated sheets

Sheet 1★★ gives children practice in identifying factors and planning a fair test. (Level 4/5)

Sheet 2★★★ asks the children to identify factors, plan a test and, with help, construct a line graph from their data. (Level 4/5)

Sheet 3★★★ asks the children to identify the factors and plan a test, make repeated measurements carefully, with help, construct a line graph from their data and draw a conclusion from the evidence. (Level 5)

Sheet 4★★★ asks the children to make predictions, plan the investigation, make a series of measurements with appropriate precision, present the data as a line graph, draw conclusions that are consistent with the evidence and suggest limitations to their evidence. (Level 5)

Sheet 5 – This is the pupil record sheet to complete for this enquiry.

Background information

Identifying factors and making predictions

By now, most children will be becoming familiar with factors they change, keep the same and observe or measure. Encourage them to talk about more factors than can be investigated in this lesson, for example, different kinds of exercise cause different rates of increase in pulse rate — how does the pulse rate return to normal after exercise?

If we ask the children to say what they think will happen to their pulse rate if they exercise, they usually say it will increase. This prediction is the most obvious feature of the expected results. The AKSIS team suggests a way to make predicting a more challenging activity. Ask them to predict what shape the graph might be and encouraging them to discuss the science behind the investigation. They do, however, need to know about line graphs before they can do this. Practice Sheet 1 is designed to support work they are doing at this stage in mathematics, relating it to the investigation in hand.

Planning what evidence to collect

In this investigation, the evidence to collect may also seem obvious to the children — pulse rate. Further thought will reveal that they should take measurements which are as accurate as possible, and to do that several repeats are needed. They have to make a comparison by calculating the difference between, before, and after exercise, and that means remembering to take the pulse rate before exercise as well as after, and to have a rest between to allow the heart rate to return to normal. They have to find a way to calculate the average of the repeated measurements and they have to record their data in a table. Those children who work out the graph from group results have, in addition, to average each person's pulse rate to plot their line graph.

Presenting results on a line graph

The tables on each of Sheets 2, 3 and 4 have headings given. These are based on the factor which is changed (the independent variable) and the factor being measured (the dependent variable). This helps the children to see how to work out which heading (axis) is which, that is, the factor which is changed forms the horizontal axis and the pulse rate measurements, the vertical axis.

Explaining what the graphs show

The children look for a pattern or relationship between the two variables, exercise and pulse rate. A clear statement is needed here. The children should mention what they changed and what they measured and the overall pattern.

I/We measured our pulse rate before and after exercise. The line graph shows that my/our pulse rate increased by (x) as we stepped up and down on a gym bench for 3 minutes. My muscles need more blood when I exercise, so my heart has to beat faster. My pulse rate shows my heart rate.

Drawing conclusions

It is clear to the children that exercise increases pulse rate and they will readily match this to their prediction. However, the evidence of a graph is limited.

For example, an individual child might say:
My pulse rate went up (by x amount) when I ran about for 3 minutes.

But 'Exercise increases pulse rate' is less secure because this is a generalisation based on the evidence of only one child.

Group graphs provide more reliable results, and a whole class graph would improve the reliability even more, allowing a generalisation to be made with more confidence.

Pulse rate

Every time your heart beats, it sends a pulse of blood, like a miniature tidal wave, racing through your arteries. You can feel these pulses where an artery is near the surface of your body, such as in your wrist. Some other pulse points are in the thumb, the neck, the crook of the elbow, the groin, the back of the knee and the ankle. The pulse rate is the same as the heart rate, so you can check how quickly your heart is pumping by measuring your pulse rate.

To find the pulse, feel with your fingers (not the thumb) on the inside of the wrist below the thumb until you can feel the pulses. You may need to press the fingers on the spot to feel the pulse.

Human pulse rate varies with age. At birth the average is 130–140 beats per minute; 110–120 at 1 year old; 90–100 by 3 years, 80–90 by 10 years and 60–80 in adults.

There are exceptions, for example, some athletes have very low pulse rates.

Name .... Date ....

Investigating pulse rate

Planning a fair test

1. You want to know what affects your pulse rate.

   Make a list of the factors that might affect it ....

   ....

   ....

2. Some children thought of this question:

   How does running for three minutes affect my pulse rate?

   What do you think should go here?

   What we will change ....

   What we will keep the same ....

   What we will measure ....

Working out averages

exercise time	pulse rate in beats per minute					
	1st time		2nd time		3rd time	
	before	after	before	after	before	after
running for 3 minutes	75	115	80	110	85	120

Work out the averages like this:

Before	After
75	115
80	110
+ 85	+ 120
= 240, divide by 3 = 80 beats	= 345, divide by 3 = 115 beats

Name .... Date ....

Keeping healthy: Investigating pulse rate

We take our pulse like this:

I think these factors could affect our pulse rate

....

....

....

Plan a test to answer this question:

How does exercising for different times affect my pulse rate?

My prediction ....

My measurements:

time exercised in minutes		pulse rate in beats per minute			
		1st time	2nd time	3rd time	average
	before				
	after				
	before				
	after				
	before				
	after				
	before				
	after				

Use this to plot the average pulse rates against time on a graph.

What did you do? ....

What does the graph show? ....

What is your conclusion? ....

Does your prediction fit the evidence? ....

Explain your conclusion ....

Name .... Date ....

Keeping healthy: Investigating pulse rate

What factors might affect your pulse rate? ....

....

My question: How does .... affect ....?

My prediction: ....

My test:

what we will change	what we will measure	what we will keep the same

Results:

time exercised in minutes		pulse rate in beats per minute			average
		1st time	2nd time	3rd time	
	before				
	after				
	before				
	after				
	before				
	after				
	before				
	after				

Show your results on a graph.

What does the graph show? ....

What is your conclusion? ....

Does your prediction fit the evidence? ....

Explain your conclusion on the back of this sheet.

Name .... Date ....

Keeping healthy: Investigating pulse rate

The factor we think could have most effect on our pulse rate is ....

....

We predict that ....

....

Our question ....

....

Our test.　Factor we will change ....

Factors we will not change ....

What we will measure ....

How we will measure the group ....

....

Our line graph will be this shape:

Results table:

Show your results on a graph.

Our interpretation of the graph ....

....

Our conclusion ....

Limitations of our work ....

....

Name .... Date ....

Keeping healthy: Investigating pulse rate

Identifying factors and making predictions.

❏ I suggested a factor that might cause pulse rate to increase. (Level 4)

❏ I identified more than one factor. (Level 5)

❏ I predicted that exercising for a certain time would increase my pulse rate. (Level 4)

❏ I also predicted the likely shape of the line graph. (Level 5)

Planning what evidence to collect

❏ I suggested when to measure the pulse rate.

❏ I also suggested that we repeat the measurements and test more than one person (Level 5)

Presenting results on a line graph

❏ I used my results and plotted points on a line graph correctly. (Level 4/5)

❏ I named the headings correctly. (Level 5)

❏ I worked out the scales with some help. (Level 5)

Name .... Date ....

Keeping healthy: Investigating pulse rate

Interpreting line graphs

- ☐ I know what my line graph shows. (Level 4)

- ☐ I described the factors we changed and measured.

- ☐ I drew a conclusion from the evidence on my graph. (Level 5)

- ☐ I matched the conclusion to my prediction.

- ☐ I changed my prediction when I saw the evidence.

- ☐ I know there are limitations to my work because it was a very small sample. (Level 5)

Life cycles: Investigating germination

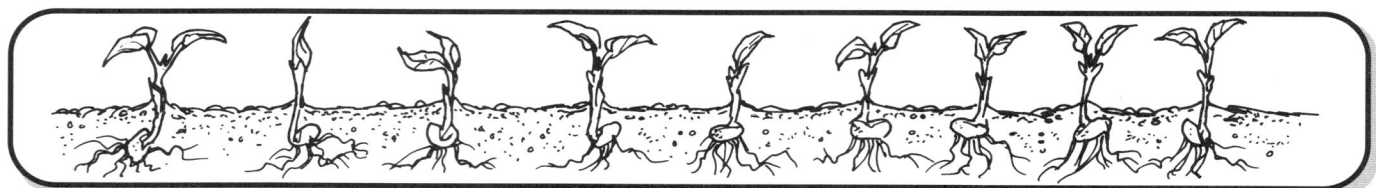

Learning objectives

Children should learn:

- that plants reproduce
- to **consider conditions** that might affect germination and **plan how to test them**
- how to **alter one factor at a time** in order to carry out a fair test
- that several seeds should be used in each set of conditions in order to **get reliable evidence**
- to **make careful observations and comparisons and use these to draw conclusions**
- that **seeds need water and warmth (but not light) for germination**.

Lesson notes

⏰ Approximate timing: 2 hours spread over several days or two lessons one week apart.

Type of scientific enquiry

This scientific enquiry gives the children the opportunity to practice their skills in planning and carrying out an enquiry within a biological context.

Many of the children will remember their work with seeds in Key Stage 1. This will, to some extent, allow them to concentrate fully on the investigative skills they are using.

Introduction

Describe a context for the investigation connected to the children's previous work on seed dispersal — It is spring and the seeds which were scattered in the autumn are beginning to germinate. What's the weather like? What are the conditions for the seeds in spring? It is warmer, etc. Share the lesson objectives with the children.

Show them a variety of seeds, including some soaked overnight in water (broad beans or peas). Ask the children to work together to examine them,

split them and see the various parts, including the cotyledon (food supply) and the embryo root and shoot. Ask them to think what they might need to begin to grow (germinate).

- What are the factors which could affect germination?
— heat, water, light, air, soil…
- What are your predictions?
— 'without water seeds will not germinate' '…seeds need all these things'.

Concentrate on heat, water and light, most children handling one variable and a few investigating two types of seed.

Decide what sort of seeds to use — peas, beans, grass seeds, sunflowers, oilseed rape,
— these all germinate within a few days; onion, carrot, parsley, for example, germinate more slowly.

Decide how many seeds — several, five; two different ones — grass and peas.

Use shallow plastic trays lined with at least two layers of kitchen paper. (They may remember which kitchen papers are the most/least absorbent from Year 3 Unit 3C.) When testing whether seeds need water, larger seeds which are to be put onto damp paper could be soaked for a few hours beforehand, (but not those to be put in dry conditions). Adequate water is needed, but not so much that the seeds are immersed in water. Soaked seeds could be used for each investigation. Discuss how to make the test fair.

Individual and group work

The children work together to plan and set up their investigations in pairs or threes. Some children may need to plan, carry out and plan again. Use Sheet 1 for those who need some practice, and/or Sheets 2, 3 and 4.

They make and record careful observations over a period of up to ten days, as appropriate. They draw conclusions from the evidence.

As the children are working, probe their thinking and ideas about enquiry skills and processes, making the skills overt and clear:

- What factor/s they have chosen?

- Whether their prediction is carefully worded and, perhaps, contains a reason

- Whether their question is one which can be tested, — is it of the Does x affect y? type — Does the amount of heat affect the germination of sunflower seeds?

- Whether their table of results is adequate and how, for example, they decided when a seed has germinated

- Whether their conclusions fit the evidence and their predictions

- How reliable they think their evidence is.

Whole class

Discuss any points which came up in general and any surprises, e.g. the seeds in the fridge germinated. Include the findings of those who tested two kinds of seeds. Ask about how the seeds germinate, what came first, if they grew at the same pace. Find out if all groups testing the same independent variable have the same results. Suggest that this makes the results more reliable. From the results the class has obtained, come to a conclusion about what their seeds need to germinate (warmth and water, but not light).

Differentiated Sc1 learning outcomes

Considering factors (the conditions)

- uses previous knowledge to identify one or more factors which might affect germination

- varies one factor whilst keeping the others the same.

Planning how to test them

- suggests growing some seeds

- suggests using a fair test.

Altering one factor at a time

- changes one factor and keeps others the same

- knows which factor they are changing, which they keep the same and which they are measuring

- plans to use two types of seed to test one factor.

Getting reliable evidence

- decides how often to observe the seeds

- also decides on a point when a seed has germinated successfully and how many seeds to use.

Makes careful observations and comparisons

- observes carefully and concentrates on signs of germination and makes relevant comments

- observes relevant features of germination, deciding when a seed has germinated, comparing the signs in each seed.

Uses these to draw conclusions

- draws a general conclusion — seeds need water…

- draws a conclusion based on the evidence from their test — our seeds need water…

- draws a conclusion based on evidence from all the tests conducted by the class. Seeds need water and warmth but not light to germinate.

Using the differentiated sheets

Sheet 1★★ gives the children practice in planning and carrying out a fair test and concluding and evaluating. Look for and, if necessary, help the children to pose questions which include the factors: Do seeds need water to germinate? or Does the amount of water affect germination of seeds? (Level 4)

Sheet 2★★★ asks the children to make suggestions about the investigation, carry out a fair test (with some help), record using a table and draw a conclusion. (Level 4/5)

Sheet 3★ provides a table for children to record their results in. (Level 3)

Sheet 4★★★ asks the children to suggest a fair test as appropriate, identify key factors, predict using scientific knowledge, design a table and record observations systematically. They draw conclusions based on the evidence, relating these to scientific knowledge. They also make more detailed notes on their observations. (Level 5)

The children should also be differentiated according to how much help they need.

Sheet 5 – This is the pupil record sheet to complete for this enquiry.

Background information

Considering conditions that might affect germination

This is an investigation to which most children will bring some scientific knowledge. This familiarity with factors that affect germination will help them to manipulate the factors more easily. Because of this they are more likely to be successful.

Altering one factor at a time (in a fair test)

Having a clear question such as 'Does light affect germination?' will help the children to concentrate on the factor to change (the independent variable) and the factor to observe (the dependent variable). They can then see that all other things within their control are not altered (the control variables).

To use an idea based on AKSIS research try this:

● List all the factors that might affect germination — heat, water, light, air, — and write each on a separate Post-it™. Write the factor to observe on its own label.

● Decide which to test — light. Put that sticky label in the 'What we will change' box on a large version of the practice sheet 1. Put the factor to observe in place. Then put the other three factors into the 'we will keep the same' boxes.

● Do it again, this time making water the factor to change — light now goes into a controlled box. Practise manipulating the factors in this way. Note that the factor to observe remains the same each time, but the other variables change. There should always be the same number of factors in the controlled boxes and only one factor as the 'star of the show'.

The children working at Level 4–5 may suggest using two species of seeds; see that they put each into the same conditions, results table and conclusions (Sheet 4).

Getting reliable evidence

For evidence to be reliable, the test should be repeatable — producing the same results. In the case of seeds, there may be some that do not germinate or germinate in a misshapen way. Some seeds take longer to germinate, even of the same sort. Knowing this will help the children to decide a sensible number to test — at least 5, perhaps 20. Secondly, it is a good idea to use a variety of seeds and thirdly, compare all the groups' results to see how well they agree. Test a conclusion by asking what, based on their results, they predict other children doing the same test, would find.

Making careful observations and comparisons and using these to draw conclusions

Children are often remarkably good at noticing tiny details and by this age will have begun to recognise what is relevant and which senses are appropriate. For example, what emerges from the seed first, what next and when. There should be plenty of room on their results tables for them to record their observations and comparisons.

Children in years 5 and 6 are beginning to correctly link cause and effect. Some will still give vague statements and others will write descriptive statements. Encourage the children to draw on their earlier experience of considering evidence and drawing conclusions. It would be very easy here to jump to the conclusion that 'all seeds need water and warmth to germinate, but not light'. In fact, some seeds do need light to germinate and others germinate better in light conditions. However, these are exceptions to the rule.

Seeds and germination

All seeds contain an embryo with the potential to grow into a mature plant similar to other members of its species. Most seeds also contain food reserves that are used during the early stages of germination. When a seed absorbs water it swells, then, after a few days, the root emerges and absorbs more water from the soil, and finally, the shoot emerges. This is the process of germination.

There are some species of plant that do not germinate in darkness, and need light to do so. Grass and lettuce germinate better in light conditions. Other seeds, coconuts, for example, need to be immersed in salt water before they can germinate, and many seeds germinate more readily in cool conditions, e.g. onions and parsley, which prefer temperatures of 10°C or below.

Name .... Date ....

Investigating germination

Planning an investigation

What factors do you think might affect germination?

....

....

Design some tests:

1. Suppose this is your question: Do seeds need light to germinate?

   Make a prediction: ....

   ....

We will change	We will observe	We will not change these factors		

2. Now pose your own question: ....

   ....

   Make a prediction: ....

   ....

We will change	We will observe	We will not change these factors		

Name .... Date ....

Investigating germination

What do you think seeds need to make them germinate?

....

....

Which one will you test? ....

What is your prediction? ....

....

A fair test

Fill in the spaces:

We will put .... seeds in .... and in ....

We will be changing the ....

We will keep these the same ....

We will watch ....

Use a table for your results

Number of seeds ....

Kind of seed ....

What happened to the seeds? ....

....

What is your conclusion? ....

....

How could you make your test better? ....

....

Name .... Date ....

Investigating germination

Day	What we noticed	How many germinated
1		
2		
3		
4		
5		
6		
7		
8		
9		
10		

Name .... Date ....

Investigating germination

Fair test using two kinds of seed

This is what we will change	This is what we will observe	This is what we will keep the same

The factors that might affect seed germination ....

....

Question ....

Prediction (include why you think this) ....

....

The kind of investigation to answer this question ....

....

Put your results in a table

Number of seeds .... Kind of seed ....

Notes on observations ....

....

Conclusion ....

Ways to improve the test ....

....

....

Name .... Date ....

Life cycles: Investigating germination

Considering factors

❑ I suggested some factors that might affect germination. (Level 4)

❑ I suggested the key factors that might affect germination. (Level 5)

Altering one factor at a time in a fair test

❑ I carried out a fair test with some help. (Level 3)

❑ I planned and carried out a fair test and changed only one factor. (Level 4)

❑ I planned and carried out a fair test on two types of seeds. (Level 5)

Getting reliable evidence

❑ I decided to use at least five seeds in my test. (Level 4)

❑ I used seeds and my partner and I agreed on the results.

❑ I used two types of seeds and looked also at others' results. (Level 5)

Name .... Date ....

Life cycles: Investigating germination

Making careful observations and comparisons

❑ I looked at my seeds every day and recorded when they started to grow. (Level 3)

❑ I also noted when the root and shoot appeared out of the seeds. (Level 4)

❑ I also decided that the seeds had germinated when both the root and the shoot showed. (Level 5)

Drawing conclusions

❑ I drew a conclusion from the evidence of my tests and those of others – our seeds need .... to germinate. (Level 4)

❑ I drew a conclusion from the evidence that different types of seeds need .... to grow. (Level 5)

Gases around us: Which soil contains most air?

Learning objectives

Children should learn:

- that soils have air trapped in them
- to **measure volumes of water carefully**
- to **recognise whether measurements need to be repeated**
- to **use their results to compare** the air trapped in different soils.

Lesson notes

 Approximate timing: 2 hours.

 Do not let children dispose of soil down sinks.

 Soil should be collected from areas free from broken glass and dog faeces. Children must wash their hands after the investigation.

Type of scientific enquiry

This Sc1 enquiry will give children the opportunity to tackle a whole investigation based on fair testing.

Introduction

Ask the children about animals that live in the soil.

- How do they breathe?

Establish that there is air trapped in soil and that there are different types of soil.

Ask how we could find out, given three types of soil, which one contained most air.

If necessary show some water soaking into soil explaining that most of the water will take up the space occupied by air trapped in the soil.

- What should we keep the same to make this a fair test?

Group work

Let groups investigate three types of soil. Children should be familiar with measuring volumes of water before tackling this investigation. (Sheet 3 goes over the technique and offers some practice in the skill.) They can start with a known volume of water and pour this slowly on to the soil until no more soaks in. Then they can see the volume of water remaining and work out how much they added. (Sheet 1) As you circulate, question the reliability of results:

- If you were to repeat the test would you get the same results?

Encourage them to try the test again and explain any difference in readings. (Sheet 2)

Whole class

Collect results from the class. If children started with common volumes of soil, there is a good opportunity to demonstrate the range of values. This shows the need for repeat readings to gain more reliable evidence from which we can be more certain of our conclusions.

Differentiated Sc1 learning outcomes

Measuring

- with help, can measure volumes of water to the nearest marked division
- can measure volumes of water to the nearest marked division
- can measure volumes of water to the nearest division.

Concluding

- uses visual comparisons to sequence the results of their tests
- with help, uses measurements to sequence the results of their tests.
- uses measurements to sequence the results of their tests.

Using the differentiated sheets

Sheet 1★★ This sheet supports children working out how much water has been absorbed into the soil.

Sheets 2★★ This sheet encourages children to repeat their tests and to explain why this is a good idea in this case. (The sheet introduces a Level 5 skill.)

Sheet 3★★ This Skill Sheet introduces the technique for measuring volumes of liquid from a measuring cylinder. (This is a Level 3/4 skill.)

Sheet 4★★ This Skill Sheet gives children the opportunity to work out how much water soaked into three types of soil, then deduce which had most air trapped in it.

Sheet 5 This is the pupil record sheet to complete for this enquiry.

Background information

Measuring

This investigation relies on children's ability to measure volumes. The use of plastic measuring cylinders will promote greater accuracy than measuring cups and jugs. Discussion of the scale used on the measuring cylinders will help before the investigation (as will an exercise based on measuring volumes of water e.g. finding the capacity of different containers).

The reliability of results can be taught here as obtaining consistent readings can be difficult with each soil sample.

Concluding

Again, the children will sequence results. To increase the demand of the exercise, children can be encouraged to look for links between the size of the particles in the soil and the volume of air trapped. Viewing the soils under magnification, using microscopes if possible, will encourage their ideas when drawing conclusions. (This is an opportunity to use your school's Intel computer microscopes.)

Soils

Soils can be classified according to the size of mineral particles in them. Sandy soils have the largest particles. At the other extreme we have clay soils with very small particles. The gaps between the coarse grains of sand in a sandy soil mean that they contain most air and water drains through this type of soil faster than a clay soil which tends to get waterlogged, because it has few gaps between its tiny particles.

Name .... Date ....

Which soil contains most air?

In our test we will pour water on to the same level of soil until no more soaks in.

We will start with 100 ml of water, then see how much we have left.

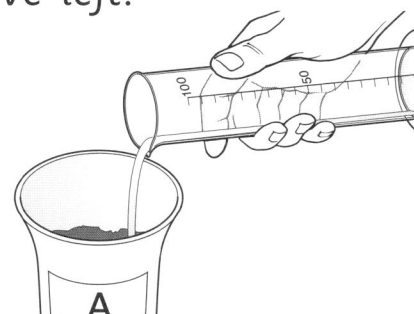 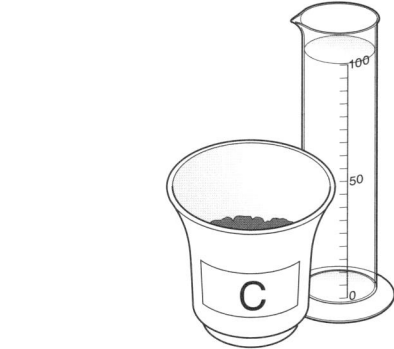

Results

Soil A

We started with 100 ml of water.

We finished with .... ml of water left.

So soil A soaked up (100 – ....) = ... ml of water.

Soil B

We started with 100 ml of water.

We finished with .... ml of water left.

So soil B soaked up (100 – ....) = ... ml of water.

Soil C

We started with 100 ml of water.

We finished with .... ml of water left.

So soil C soaked up (100 – ....) = ... ml of water.

Name .... Date ....

Which soil contains most air?

Results

Record your results in this table:

Volume of water soaked into the soil (ml)					
Soil A		Soil B		Soil C	
1st test	2nd test	1st test	2nd test	1st test	2nd test

I had to repeat my measurements because ....

....

....

Conclusion

From my results I can see that soil .... has most air trapped in it.

The order of the soils is:

1. .... (most air trapped)

2. ....

3. ....

Name .... Date ....

Measuring volumes of water

When you read the volume of water in a measuring cylinder:

1. always get your eye level with the surface of the water

2. read to the nearest mark that is level with the bottom of the curve on the surface of the water.

The curve at the surface of the water is called the meniscus.

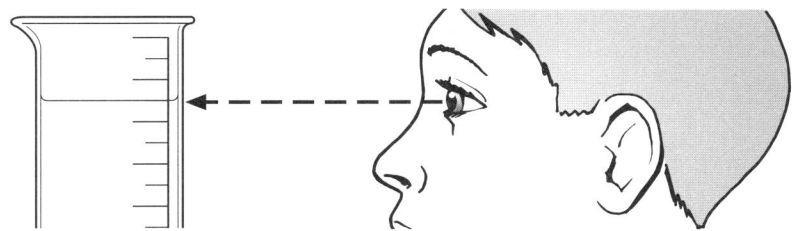

Read the volume of water in these four measuring cylinders:

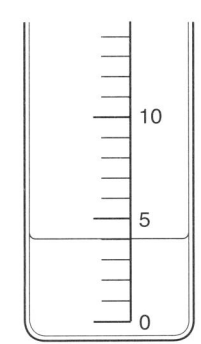

.... ml

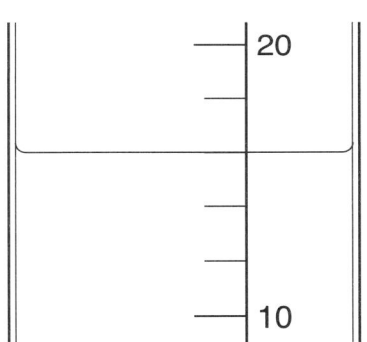

.... ml

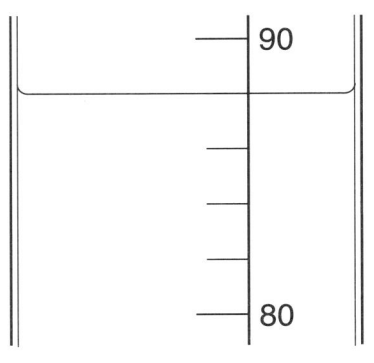

.... ml

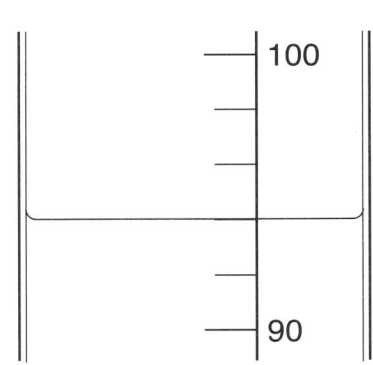

.... ml

Name .... Date ....

Which soil contains most air?

A group poured water on to the same level of soil until no more soaked in.

They started with 100ml of water, then saw how much was left.

Results

Volume of water (ml)					
Soil A		Soil B		Soil C	
Before	After	Before	After	Before	After
100	75	100	67	100	59

a) Use the results to fill in the table below:

Soil	Volume of water soaked in (ml)
A	
B	
C	

b) Put the three soils in order, with the one containing most air first:

1. .... 2. .... 3. ....

Name .... Date ....

Which soil contains most air?

Measuring

☐ I can measure volumes of water to the nearest marked division. (Level 3)

☐ I can take a series of measurements of water when seeing how much air is trapped in soils. (Level 4)

☐ I can measure accurately the volumes of water in the soils investigation, working out how much water has soaked in, and repeating measurements to get more reliable results. (Level 5)

Concluding

☐ I can put my results in order based on how much water soaked into the soils, and explain how I decided on the order. (Level 3)

☐ I can use the work we have done in science to explain the pattern in my results. (Level 4/5)

Changing state:
What affects how quickly water evaporates?

Nelson Thornes Ref: PS Kit 5.4.2

Learning objectives

Children should learn:

- to **turn ideas into a form that that can be investigated**, to **make a prediction** and **decide what evidence to collect**
- to **construct a fair test**
- to **make careful measurements, recording them in tables and graphs**
- to **identify trends in results and use these to draw conclusions, indicating whether the results support the prediction**
- to **explain conclusions in terms of scientific knowledge and understanding**.

Lesson notes

⏱ Approximate timing: 1.5 hours initially (continuing over several days)

Type of scientific enquiry

This Sc1 enquiry will give children the opportunity to tackle a whole investigation based on fair testing.

Introduction

Ask children to think about washing that is hanging out to dry.

- What happens to the water?

To prompt the factors that affect evaporation ask:

- What affects how quickly the washing dries?
- Record children's ideas, then ask them to frame a question to investigate one particular factor. If necessary start off the question with 'How does …?'
- Ask children to predict the answer to their question.

Sheets 1 and 2 will provide a structure for these activities.

Group work

The two factors that children commonly investigate are temperature (although this is difficult to control, apart from inside a fridge) and surface area (using differently shaped containers for the same volumes of water). Children can investigate the air flow over the surface with the aid of battery powered fans or by leaving one bowl of water in a draughty place (again difficult to control).

Where possible let children investigate their own suggestions if resources allow.

This will be an investigation that runs for several days. Sheets 3, 4 and 5 provide possible formats for tables to record results. To produce line graphs, higher attaining children should monitor their tests each day. Less demanding bar charts will be produced by considering 'before' (at the start) and 'after' (at the end) measurements.

Children usually measure the rate of evaporation by the volume of water remaining or the height of the water in containers of the same dimensions. Borrowing a sensitive balance from a local secondary school can produce results much more quickly.

Whole class

Draw together the results after a week and discuss findings. Ask children to check their predictions against the evidence gathered and then to explain their conclusions.

Evaluate the investigation, looking for ways that the method(s) could be improved to provide stronger evidence.

Differentiated Sc1 learning outcomes

Questioning and predicting

- with help, poses a question to investigate and predicts what will happen
- poses a question to investigate and predicts what will happen, explaining their reasoning.

Planning

- with help, decides what to change, what to measure and what to keep the same
- decides what to change, what to measure and what to keep the same.

Recording

- with help, fills in a table of results and displays them on a bar chart
- fills in a table of results and displays them on a bar chart
- designs and fills in a table of results and displays them on a line graph.

Concluding

- uses visual comparisons to sequence the results of their tests
- with help, uses measurements to sequence the results of their tests
- uses measurements to sequence the results of their tests

- uses measurements to sequence the results of their tests and explains why their results are consistent with their prediction.

Using the differentiated sheets

Sheet 1★★★ This sheet allows children to generate the key factors influencing evaporation, to choose one factor to investigate, and finally to make and explain a prediction. (Level 5 skills required for unsupported work.)

Sheet 2★★★ This sheet gives children the opportunity to plan their own fair test. (Level 4/5)

Sheets 3 and 4★ These sheets provide the table to record results in — Sheet 3 if children are measuring the height of water in containers of equal dimensions or Sheet 4 if they are measuring volumes of water left. (Level 4 — producing series of measurements in tables.)

Sheet 5★★★ This sheet provides a format for recording all results in one table and gives support for concluding and evaluating their investigation. (Level 4/5)

Sheet 6★★ This Skill Sheet requires children to read scales, record results in a table, use the results to sequence the order of evaporation and to speculate on the shapes of the containers under investigation. (Level 4)

Sheet 7 This is the pupil record sheet to complete for this enquiry.

Background information

Questioning

By generating the factors that affect how quickly washing dries, children have formed the basis of their questions to investigate. The degree of support different children will need in turning these into a question will vary, often depending on their literacy skills. However, most children can do this exercise once an example of a question to investigate has been demonstrated.

Planning

Most children will be able to respond to questions about which things should be kept the same to make this a fair test. Others will by now be familiar with the template of a fair test and will be deciding themselves what to change, what to measure and what to keep the same with the help of a planning frame.

Recording

The rate of evaporation is slow, so without accurate instruments to measure the mass of water remaining, the investigation will require measurements and recording over a period of time. Children enjoy these ongoing investigations in which a systematic way of recording measurements becomes even more important.

Graphs can be used to display results, the most demanding showing a line for each set of conditions investigated on the same axes. Support will be needed if appropriate measurements have been collected to produce such a graph (although some children might have experience of this type of graph from Unit 4C in which they investigated thermal insulators).

Concluding

Children can check if their results support their predictions made at the start of the investigation. They can look for patterns and try to explain these using their knowledge of changes in state. For example, it is easier for the water to change into a gas and escape from the container with the wide opening.

Encourage the wording of pattern recognition. For example, the higher the temperature, the faster the water evaporates.

Evaporation

When the particles of a liquid escape from its surface as a gas (below the boiling point of the liquid), the liquid evaporates. In any liquid the particles are slipping and sliding over and around each other. The particles will have a range of energies. Some of the particles at the surface will have enough energy to escape the attractive forces of neighbouring particles and will break free of the liquid into the air.

The higher the temperature the more particles have enough energy to escape from the liquid and the rate of evaporation will increase.

Name .... Date ....

What affects how quickly water evaporates?

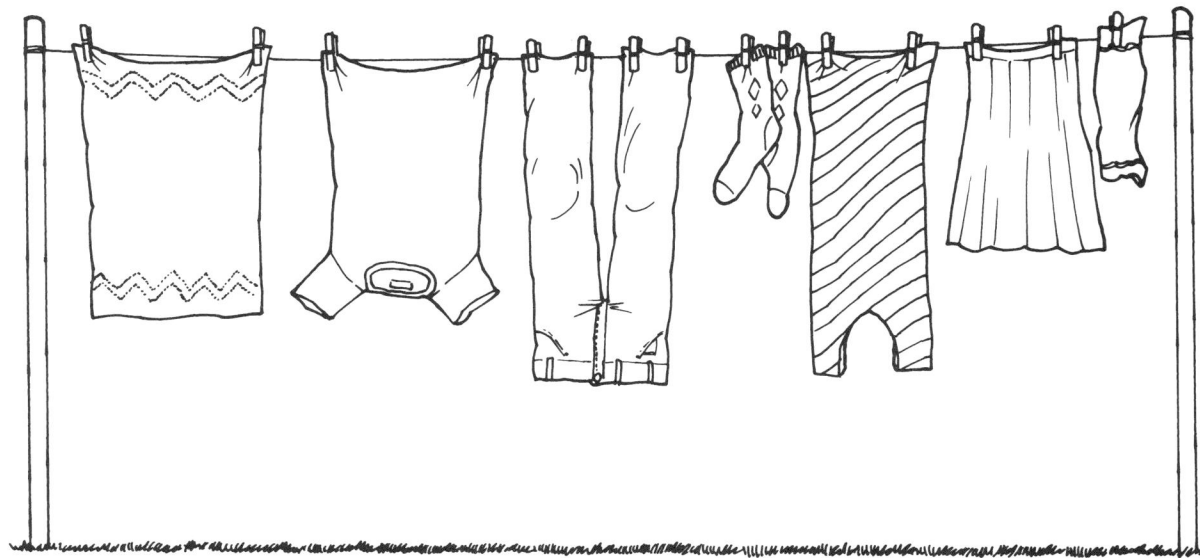

I think these things will affect how quickly water evaporates:

....

....

....

....

Choose one thing from your list above to investigate.

I would like to find out the answer to this question:

How does .... affect how quickly
water evaporates?

I predict that ....

....

because ....

....

Name .... Date ....

What affects how quickly water evaporates?

Plan

To find out the answer to my question:

How does .... affect how quickly water evaporates?

We will change: ....

We will measure: .... each day.

We will keep these things the same: ....

....

....

Here are the details of my plan: ....

....

....

....

....

....

Name .... Date ....

What affects how quickly water evaporates?

Put your results in these tables:

This water is ....

Number of days	Height of water (mm)

This water is ....

Number of days	Height of water (mm)

Name .... Date ....

What affects how quickly water evaporates?

Put your results in these tables:

This water is ....

Number of days	Volume of water (ml)

This water is ....

Number of days	Volume of water (ml)

Name .... Date ....

What affects how quickly water evaporates?

Put your results in this table:

Time (days)	Volume of water (ml)			
	Container 1	Container 2	Container 3	Container 4

Show your results on a graph.

Conclusion

From my results I can see that my prediction is ....

This is because ....

....

....

....

Evaluation

We could get better results by ....

....

....

Name .... Date ....

What affects how quickly water evaporates?

A group left the same volume of water in differently shaped bowls.

After a week they measured the volumes again and got the results below:

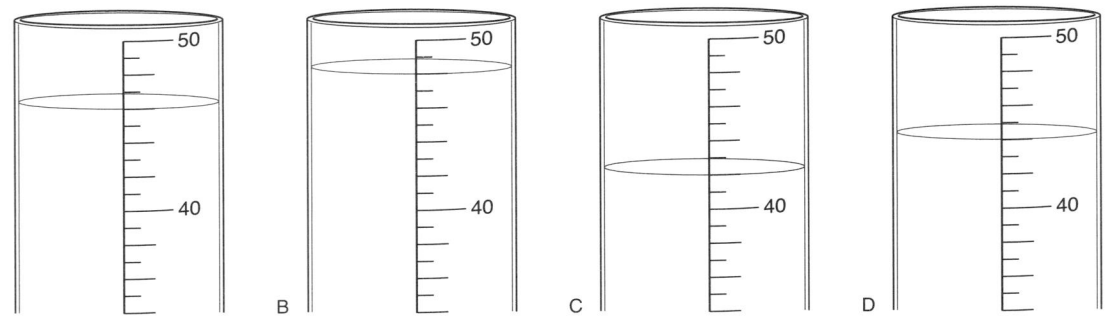

a) Put their results into the table below:

Bowl	Volume of water left (ml)
A B C D	

c) Put the bowls into order:

1. .... (water evaporates most quickly)

2. ....

3. ....

4. ....

Try to explain these results by drawing what each bowl might look like on the back of this sheet.

Name .... Date ....

What affects how quickly water evaporates?

Planning

❏ With help, I can plan what to change, what to measure and what to keep the same to carry out a fair test. (Level 3)

❏ I can plan what to change, what to measure and what to keep the same to carry out a fair test. (Level 4)

❏ I can list all the factors that might affect how quickly water evaporates. Then I can plan what to change, what to measure and what to keep the same to carry out a fair test. (Level 5)

Concluding

❏ I can check whether my results support my prediction or not. (Level 2)

❏ I can put my results in order based on how quickly the water evaporated, and explain how I decided on the order. (Level 3)

❏ I can use the work we have done in science to explain the pattern in my results. (Level 4/5)

Interdependence and adaptation:
Using keys to identify and group living things

Nelson Thornes Ref: PS Kit 4.2.4 and 6.1.3

Learning objectives

Children should learn:

● **to (make and) use keys** to identify animals and plants in a local habitat

Note that this activity also includes work on assigning vertebrates to groups.

Lesson notes

⏱ Approximate timing: 2 hours with extra time to revisit a local habitat.
Arrange to revisit a habitat familiar to the children.

Type of scientific enquiry

This enquiry gives the children the opportunity to identify and classify some local plants and animals, using and making keys.

Introduction

Start by asking the children what they remember about the habitat they will be revisiting and the plants and animals living in the various habitats.

Explore their understanding of 'habitat' and of how living things depend on each other and the environment to live. Remind them of their work in Year 4 on identification and using keys — when they used two types of key to identify some invertebrates (they may have used a branching database program in addition).

Individual and group work

The children rehearse the skills involved in using a key, using Sheets 1, 2 or 3.

Whole class

Take the children through the process of making a key:

● Take four shells — cockle, mussel, razor shell and whelk. Make sure the bivalves are complete with both shells. Talk about the important features of each shell — whether there are one or two shells per animal — the colour, surface, shape.

● Then, choose a characteristic which only one of them has: only one shell, and you have the first question.

● Make up a second question which, again, only one of the three remaining shells has: a purplish-black shell. Carry on in this way until you have identified each type of shell — texture and shape of the shell. Where possible, add an extra question to make sure of each identification.

● Construct the key with the whole class, pointing out how the questions are designed to lead towards one physical feature that is unique to the animal and so to each organism.

Individual and group work.

Out in the field, ask the children to collect some things and make notes about others — collect invertebrates — spiders, beetles, centipedes, etc.; leaves from trees; or make notes about other organisms which may not be collected — birds, or flowers; for example, four blue, red or yellow flowers, noting the special features — number of petals, petal/leaf shape, seed head, position of the leaves, etc.

Back in the classroom, ask the children to identify their organisms from reference sources and then construct keys to help others to identify them. Use the obvious physical features and, if appropriate, information in the books to pull out differences between the organisms.

Whole class

Try out some of the children's keys with the class; encourage them to comment on each others' work.

Either at this stage in the lesson, or earlier, some children may attempt Sheet 4 using a key to identify amphibians and reptiles.

Differentiated Sc1 learning outcomes

Using keys to identify animals and plants

● uses a simple yes/no key for identifying organisms

● uses a simple branching key to identify four invertebrates

● uses a branching key to identify four skulls of small mammals

● uses a branching key of greater complexity to identify eight European amphibians and reptiles.

Making keys to identify plants and animals

● identifies several important differences between the organisms

● constructs questions with 'yes' or 'no' answers in a branching key which successfully identifies each organism

● knows about the organisation of invertebrates into groups through using a branching key to identify them.

Using the differentiated sheets

Sheet 1★★ asks the children to use a simple 'yes'/'no' key and a simple branching key to identify four different organisms — ant, worm, ladybird and spider. (Level 4)

Sheet 2★★ asks the children to use a simple branching key to identify four skulls of small mammals from an owl pellet. (Level 4)

Sheet 3★★★ asks the children to use a more complex branching key to identify eight amphibians and reptiles. (Level 4)

Sheet 4★★★ asks the children to use reference sources to distinguish between amphibians and reptiles using a key.

Sheet 5 is a record of learning for the children to fill in.

Background information

Using and making identification keys

A key consists of information arranged so that an unknown species can be identified. Most keys work by asking questions or matching pictures, to which the response is either 'yes' or 'no'. This either allows the organism to be identified or narrows down the choice through a branching key. Computer database keys are constructed on this principle.

Classification

The living world can be divided into five main groups or kingdoms. The two main ones are animals and plants and the three other kingdoms are simple organisms – bacteria, protists and fungi. In some methods of classification the simple organisms can be included in either of the main animal or plant groups.

Animals and plants are further divided into groups where all the members show strong likenesses to each other: animals are sub-divided into invertebrates and vertebrates, plants into those which do not have flowers and those which do. These are further divided into smaller and smaller classifications, the lowest of which is the species.

The process of classification continues to develop, as evolutionary relationships between organisms are clarified. Ideally, all the forms gathered together in one stage of classification have evolved from one ancestral species.

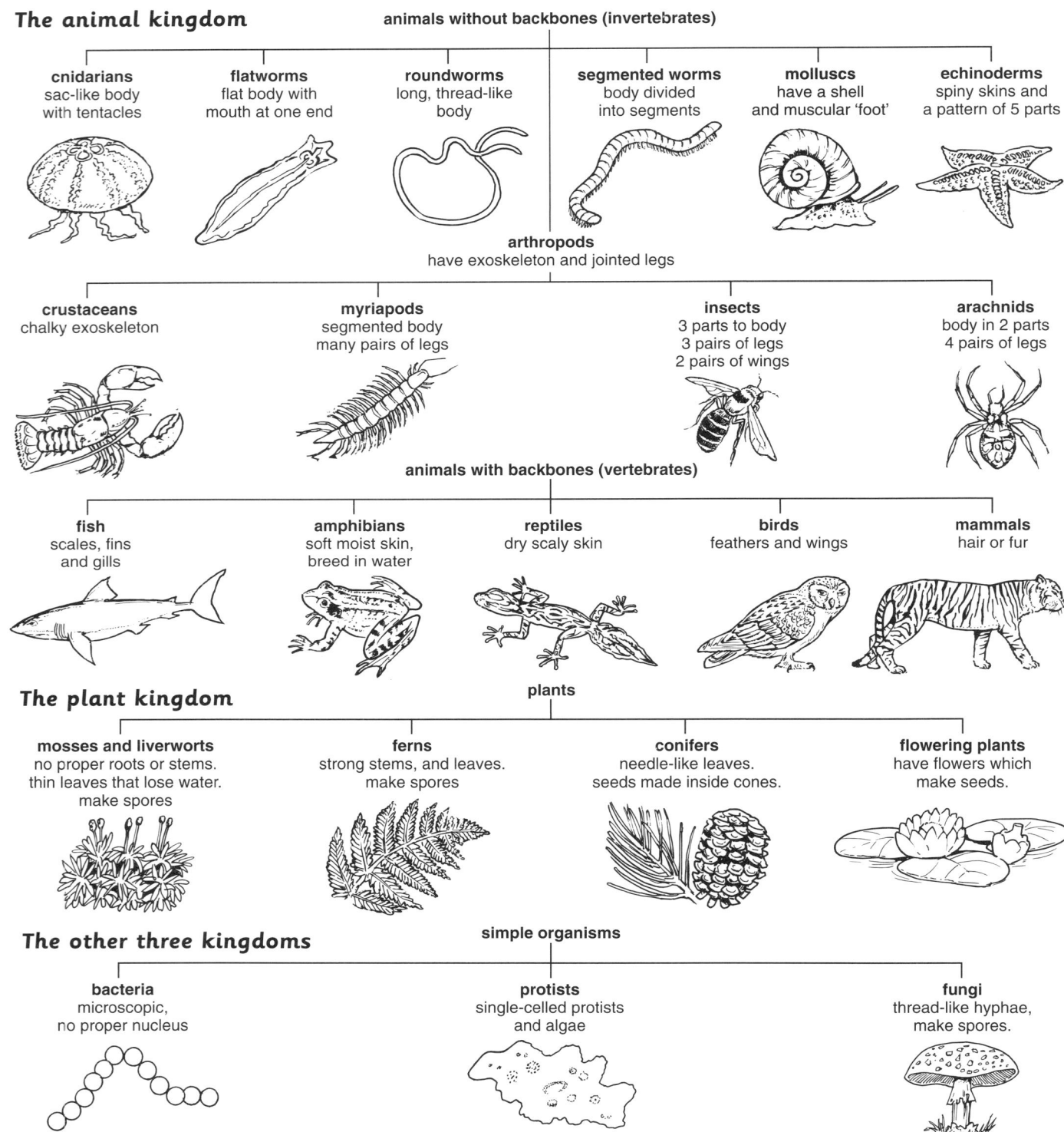

The animal kingdom

animals without backbones (invertebrates)

cnidarians
sac-like body
with tentacles

flatworms
flat body with
mouth at one end

roundworms
long, thread-like
body

segmented worms
body divided
into segments

molluscs
have a shell
and muscular 'foot'

echinoderms
spiny skins and
a pattern of 5 parts

arthropods
have exoskeleton and jointed legs

crustaceans
chalky exoskeleton

myriapods
segmented body
many pairs of legs

insects
3 parts to body
3 pairs of legs
2 pairs of wings

arachnids
body in 2 parts
4 pairs of legs

animals with backbones (vertebrates)

fish
scales, fins
and gills

amphibians
soft moist skin,
breed in water

reptiles
dry scaly skin

birds
feathers and wings

mammals
hair or fur

The plant kingdom

plants

mosses and liverworts
no proper roots or stems.
thin leaves that lose water.
make spores

ferns
strong stems, and leaves.
make spores

conifers
needle-like leaves.
seeds made inside cones.

flowering plants
have flowers which
make seeds.

The other three kingdoms

simple organisms

bacteria
microscopic,
no proper nucleus

protists
single-celled protists
and algae

fungi
thread-like hyphae,
make spores.

Name .... Date ....

Using keys to name invertebrates

Here are two different keys. Use them to name these animals:

Key 1

1. Does it have legs?
   No. It's an **earthworm**
   Yes. Go to 2.

2. Does it have eight legs?
   Yes. It's a **spider**
   No. Go to 3.

3. Does it have spots?
   Yes. It's a **ladybird**
   No. It's an **ant**.

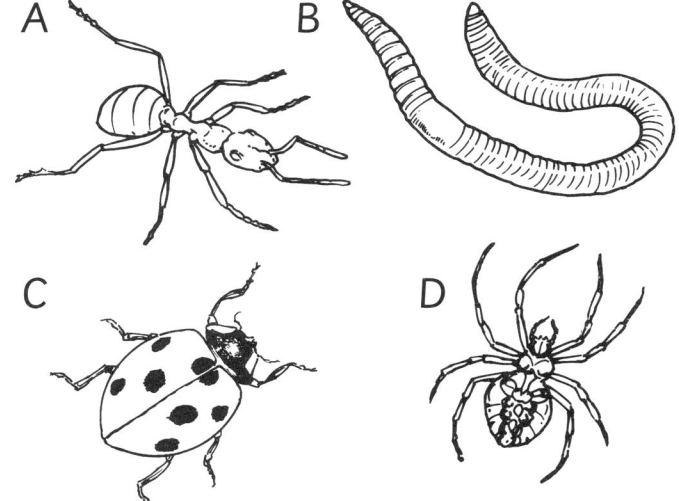

A ....   B ....   C ....   D ....

Key 2

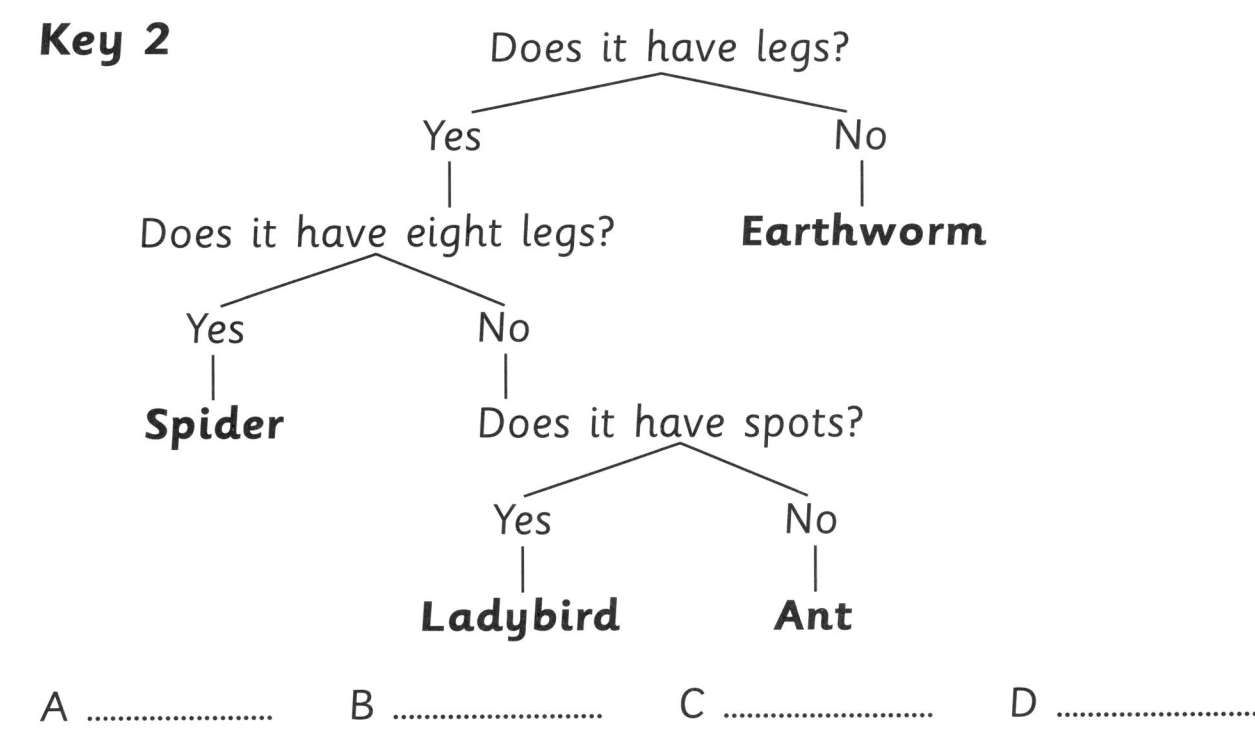

A ....   B ....   C ....   D ....

Name .... Date ....

Using a key to identify animals owls eat

Owls eat small animals but cannot digest all parts of them. They regurgitate skulls, some bones and fur or feathers in owl pellets. Use the key to name the skulls found in some owl pellets.

A   B   C   D

Red-tipped teeth

Does the skull have teeth?

Yes   No

Are the teeth evenly spaced with no gaps?

Yes   No

Does it have short incisors?

Yes   No

Mole

Does it have teeth with red tips?

Yes

Shrew

Does it have a beak?

Yes

Bird

Is the top of the skull flat?

Yes   No

Rat   **Rabbit**

Name .... Date ....

Using a key to identify some reptiles and amphibians

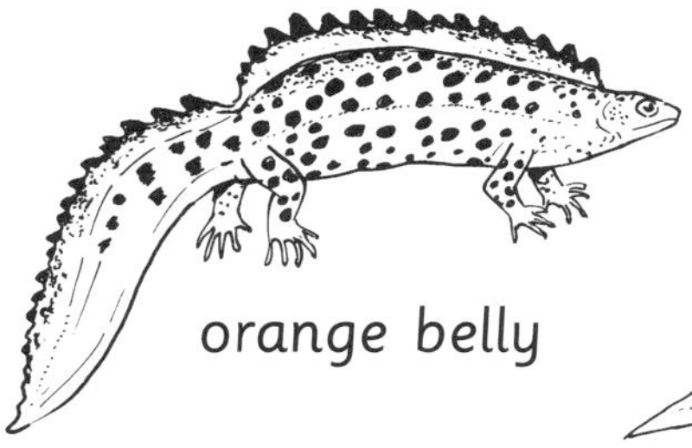

orange belly

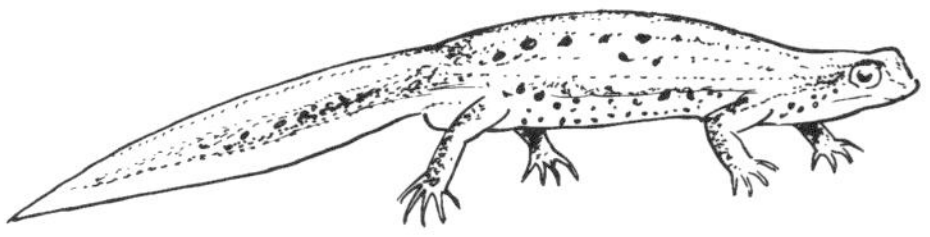

Does it have legs?

No ——————————————— Yes

Zig-zag pattern down the back?

Yes

Adder

Big bulging eyes?

Yes ——————————— No

Bumpy warty skin?

Crest along back?

Yes   No

**Common
toad**

Smooth skin?

Yes

**Common
frog**

Yes   No

Orange belly?   Webbed feet?

Yes   Yes   No

**Crested
newt**   **Palmate
newt**   **Smooth
newt**

Name .... Date ....

Amphibian or reptile?

Use reference sources and this key to find out:

Are they vertebrates?

Yes

Are they cold-blooded?

Yes

Do they have dry skin and scales or bony plates?

Yes   No

Do most lay their eggs
on land or carry live
young?

Yes

Reptiles

eg Turtles, tortoises,
snakes, lizards,
crocodiles and alligators

Do they have moist
skin, mostly smooth,
sometimes warty?

Yes

Do they lay their eggs in water?

Yes

Amphibians

eg Newts, frogs, toads

Write any other differences you found here: ....

....

....

....

Name .... Date ....

Interdependence and adaptation:
Using and making keys to identify organisms

Using keys to identify animals and plants

❑ I can use a simple yes/no key for identifying organisms

❑ I can use a simple branching key to identify four invertebrates

❑ I can use a branching key to identify four skulls of small mammals

❑ I can use a branching key to identify eight European amphibians and reptiles. (Level 4)

Making keys to identify plants and animals

❑ I can identify several important differences between the organisms

❑ I can construct questions with 'yes' or 'no' answers in a branching key that identifies each organism

❑ I know about the organisation of two vertebrate groups through using a branching key to identify the differences between them.

Micro-organisms: What does yeast need to grow?

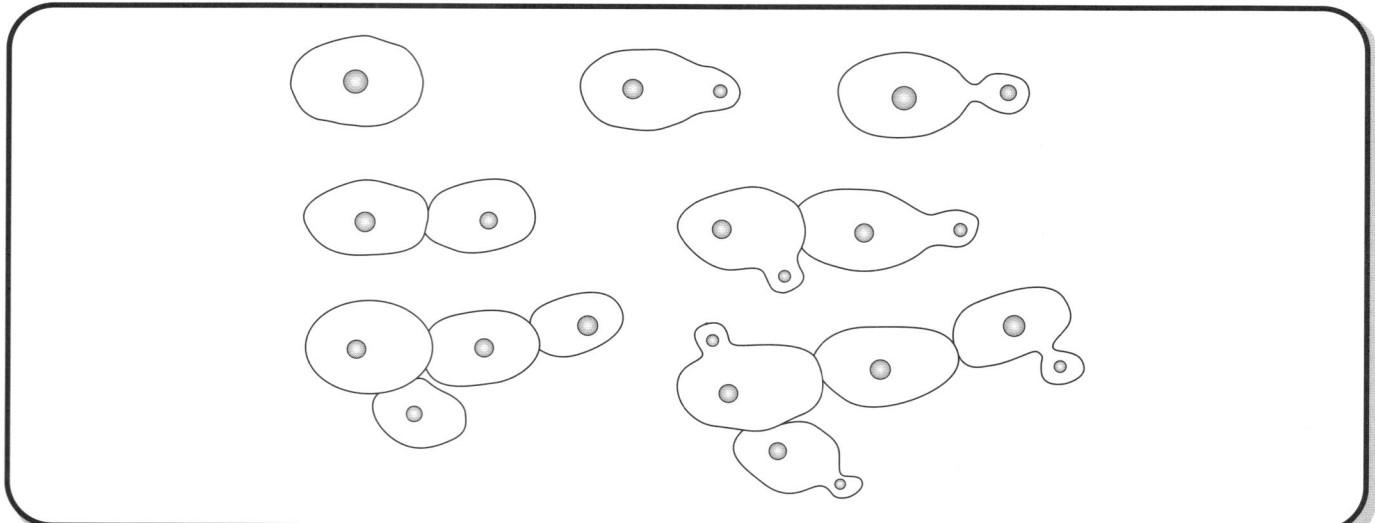

Learning objectives

Children should learn:

● that micro-organisms feed and grow

● to **make suggestions** about what yeast needs to grow

● to **make careful observations** and compare these in order **to draw conclusions** about the effect of yeast on dough

● to **explain conclusions using scientific knowledge and understanding**.

Lesson notes

 Approximate timing 2 hours

Prepare bread dough, some with and some without yeast, timed to finish rising around the start of the lesson. About half an hour before the lesson, make a mixture of yeast, sugar and warm water according to the instructions and leave it to activate.

Type of scientific enquiry

This Sc1 enquiry gives children the opportunity to plan and carry out a full investigation, including a fair test.

Introduction

Show the children some yeast in various forms — fresh, pelleted and powdered. Ask them what they know about it — what we use it for; explain what it is and how it reproduces. Ask if they think it is living.

Explain the main objective of the lesson — to find out what yeast needs to grow. Ask them to think about this as you show them the effect of yeast on the bread dough. Put it to bake. Without telling them what is in it, show them the mixture of yeast, water and sugar which is foaming nicely and explain that it is making new yeast cells and giving off a gas in the bubbles. This will help them to see what to expect, what their evidence will be. Ask how this shows that yeast is a living micro-organism.

Let the children read the instructions for using yeast on the various packets. Ask them to think about what plants need to grow or seeds need to germinate and to use these clues to suggest what yeast might need to grow.

Predictions — Yeast needs/does not need warmth/light/sugar to grow.

Questions which can be tested:

1. Does yeast need light to grow?
2. Does sugar make yeast grow?
3. Does temperature affect how well yeast grows?

Predictions —
If we keep yeast in the dark, it will not grow because plants need light to grow well.

Yeast with sugar will grow, but not without sugar because sugar is food and all living things need food.

Yeast will grow in warm water but not in cold or hot water. I think this is because organisms need some warmth to grow but not too much.

Individual and group work

The children plan fair tests to answer their question. To provide corroborating evidence, ensure that more than one pair or small group does each investigation.

Use Sheets 1 to 4. For tests 1 and 2 above, put the mixture in a clear beaker and watch for a foam forming on the top — the more foam, the more growth.

For test 3, some children could try putting the mixtures into small, clear, drinks bottles with well-stretched balloons over the neck. These will inflate slightly as the gas produced by the yeast increases. In this test, use water at three different temperatures — cold, 5°C or less; warm, about 37°C; and hot, above 60°C. Leave them for about 20 minutes to half an hour in a temperature of about 23°C or according to the instructions. (The yeast will go on producing bubbles for much longer than this if required.)

 If the gas is produced quickly, ease the balloon slightly to prevent it blowing off.

The children watch what happens, observing carefully, looking for changes in the mixtures and using all appropriate senses. They have an opportunity to write freely about their observations. Discuss the children's ideas about what is happening and what it means.

The children interpret their findings and draw conclusions. If appropriate, leave the explanations for later.

At convenient times, show them the texture of the baked bread and explain how the holes are made. Some of the children may look at yeast growing under a binocular microscope on 8×–10× magnification.

Whole class

Discuss each aspect of the investigations. Begin with their predictions — were they valid? Ask individuals to describe their test and results, encourage the children to ask each other questions and where appropriate, corroborate or challenge their results. Discuss the basis for their conclusions; work towards generalisations — yeast needs sugar (food) and warmth to grow, it does not need light. Ask the children to try to explain verbally what is happening — yeast grows and reproduces when it has sugar/warmth/both sugar and warmth. Living things grow, excrete and reproduce, so this shows that yeast

is living. Ask them to think carefully about their explanations, discuss them and record them on Sheets 2 to 4.

Differentiated Sc1 learning outcomes

Making suggestions about what yeast needs to grow

- puts forward their own idea
- makes a prediction based on knowledge about what plants and/or animals need to grow (uses scientific knowledge)
- predicts that yeast needs food (sugar) and warmth to grow.

Observing

- makes use of several senses
- notices relevant details, identifying similarities and differences
- discerns the order in which events take place.

Drawing conclusions

- interprets results by linking events together
- identifies a pattern in their observations
- ensures that the pattern or association is checked against all the data
- shows caution in making assumptions about their conclusion
- draws a valid conclusion from their evidence.

Explaining

- makes a statement of the circumstances — yeast does not need light to grow
- links cause and effect in an explanation — the sugar helped the yeast to grow; some heat is necessary for the yeast to grow well
- offers an explanation involving an applied principle — sugar helped the yeast to grow because it is their food.

Using the differentiated sheets

Sheet 1★★ gives the children practice in predicting, observing and drawing conclusions. (Level 3/4)

Sheet 2★★ gives the children a full outline to plan and carry out an investigation. (Level 4)

Sheet 3★★★ gives the children an outline with fewer details and more decisions to make (Level 4)

Sheet 4★★★ gives the children the opportunity for extended writing within a suggested framework. (Level 5)

Sheet 5 is a sheet for children to record their Sc1 skills in this investigation.

Background information

Making suggestions about what yeast needs to grow

Behind every prediction is some previous knowledge about the answer to the question. At this stage, the children are becoming better at using their scientific and everyday knowledge about how things behave. For example, in this investigation, the children will know some of the needs of all living things, such as food, and of some living things, light, warmth. If they also read the instructions about how to use yeast, they will see that sugar is needed, so they will link the two ideas and suggest that yeast needs sugar, perhaps adding 'as food to make it grow'. Their past experience with predicting and encouragement from the teacher will suggest that assumptions should be made with caution; the pattern may not apply in this case (and that is why they are doing the test). They should also be able to distinguish a prediction from a guess, which cannot be justified in terms of the evidence of previous learning.

Observing

Using the appropriate senses to note details and make comparisons between objects is something most children enjoy and are good at. To observe events, noting changes, differences and the order in which the events occur, are important skills they will be developing at this stage. This is 'observation in action' — involving careful observation.

Interpreting findings

This involves putting results together so that patterns or relationships between them can be seen. Questions such as — Does yeast need light to grow? Does yeast need sugar to grow? Does warmth affect how well yeast grows? — contain the factors involved and indicate where to look for patterns and relationships.

Drawing a general conclusion or generalisation from the evidence needs care, because it could suggest that this relationship is not only found in this particular investigation, but would be true in other cases, too. So the children will need corroborative evidence from others' tests and their knowledge of the uses we make of yeast in bread, beer and wine. It is important to check a pattern against all available evidence.

Drawing a conclusion on the effect of heat on the rate of growth of yeast is justified only if there are at least three different conditions — cold, warm and hot.

Explaining

In science the term 'explaining' does not imply certainty. Scientific knowledge is tentative, open to contradiction and/or development. Children's explanations are best offered in such an atmosphere — as suggestions, attempts, leaps of the imagination, incomplete offerings that attempt to suggest how things are as they are. A useful explanation links cause and effect and explores how a general principle applies in the circumstances.

Yeast

Yeasts are single-celled, microscopic fungi found in all parts of the world in the soil and in organic matter. For example, they occur naturally as a white covering (a bloom) on grapes and other fruit. They are produced commercially for use in baking, brewing and wine-making. They grow and reproduce by 'budding', where an outgrowth from a cell enlarges, separates from the parent and lives independently. Sometimes clusters of attached cells can be seen under a microscope. Yeast needs food and water to grow. Enzymes in the yeast break down sugar into carbon dioxide and alcohol (ethanol) in the absence of oxygen, which makes energy available for their life processes. This is called anaerobic respiration.

In baking, yeast is used to make the dough 'rise' as a result of the carbon dioxide bubbles (which are tasteless and harmless) given off before the bread is baked. The heat kills the yeast, leaving the bubbles held in place by the gluten in the flour. They expand in the heat of the oven.

Name .... Date ....

Investigating yeast

1. A Fair test

Some children asked — Does yeast need sugar to grow?

Group 1 planned like this:

We changed: *the sugar, the temperature*
We kept the same: *the amount of water and the amount of yeast*
We observed: *changes in the mixture*

Group 2 planned like this:

We changed: *the sugar*
We kept the same: *the amount and temperature of the water and the amount of yeast*
We observed: *changes in the mixture*

Which one is not a fair test? Say why you think so.

....

2. Here are the results from the group that did a fair test:

A foam came on the top of the beaker of yeast, water and sugar. There was no foam in the beaker without sugar.

One group concluded that: *'Yeast makes a foam when it grows. The beaker with foam has sugar in it. The beaker with no sugar has no foam, so the yeast is not growing. So yeast needs sugar to grow.'*
But another group said *'Yeast can't grow, it is not living. The bubbles are from the sugar in the warm water.'*

Which one is correct? Say why you think so.

....

....

3. Tick the evidence the group should use to draw a conclusion.

☐ The results of their test
☐ The results of other groups' tests
☐ What the instructions on the packets of yeast say
☐ The results of another test on just sugar and water
☐ All of these.

Give a reason. ....

....

Name .... Date ....

Investigating yeast

My question is: ....

(Check — is it a question that you can test?)

I predict that: ....

because ....

This is a fair test.

I changed ....

I kept these the same: ....

I observed ....

(Check — have you only changed one factor and kept others the same?)

This is what I observed happening: ....

....

....

(Check — have you looked several times and written down the order in which things happened?)

This is what the results mean: ....

....

(Check — have you made a link between what happened and what you changed?)

My conclusion: ....

(Check — have you used evidence from other children's tests to make your conclusion better?)

My explanation: ....

....

(Check — have you thought about what you know already about living things to help you explain?)

Name .... Date ....

What affects how quickly water evaporates?

Put your results in this table:

Time (days)	Volume of water (ml)			
	Container 1	Container 2	Container 3	Container 4

Show your results on a graph.

Conclusion

From my results I can see that my prediction is ....

This is because ....

....

....

....

Evaluation

We could get better results by ....

....

....

Name .... Date ....

What affects how quickly water evaporates?

A group left the same volume of water in differently shaped bowls.

After a week they measured the volumes again and got the results below:

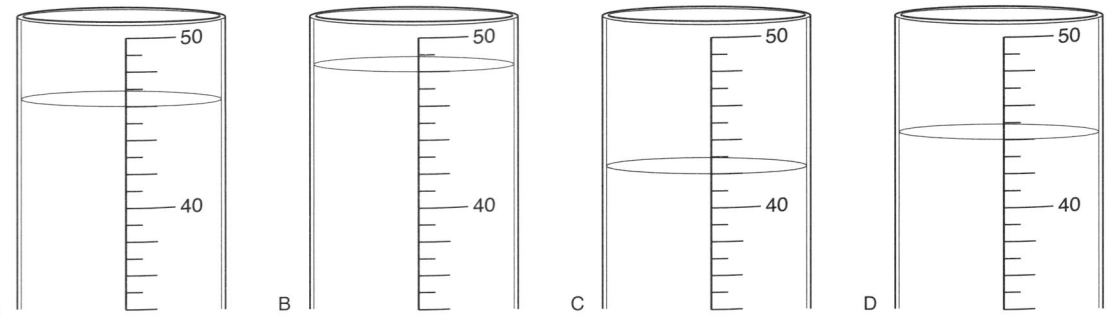

a) Put their results into the table below:

Bowl	Volume of water left (ml)
A B C D	

c) Put the bowls into order:

1. .... (water evaporates most quickly)

2. ....

3. ....

4. ....

Try to explain these results by drawing what each bowl might look like on the back of this sheet.

Name .... Date ....

What affects how quickly water evaporates?

Planning

☐ With help, I can plan what to change, what to measure and what to keep the same to carry out a fair test. (Level 3)

☐ I can plan what to change, what to measure and what to keep the same to carry out a fair test. (Level 4)

☐ I can list all the factors that might affect how quickly water evaporates. Then I can plan what to change, what to measure and what to keep the same to carry out a fair test. (Level 5)

Concluding

☐ I can check whether my results support my prediction or not. (Level 2)

☐ I can put my results in order based on how quickly the water evaporated, and explain how I decided on the order. (Level 3)

☐ I can use the work we have done in science to explain the pattern in my results. (Level 4/5)

Interdependence and adaptation: Using keys to identify and group living things

Nelson Thornes Ref: PS Kit 4.2.4 and 6.1.3

Learning objectives

Children should learn:

- **to (make and) use keys** to identify animals and plants in a local habitat

Note that this activity also includes work on assigning vertebrates to groups.

Lesson notes

⏱ Approximate timing: 2 hours with extra time to revisit a local habitat.

Arrange to revisit a habitat familiar to the children.

Type of scientific enquiry

This enquiry gives the children the opportunity to identify and classify some local plants and animals, using and making keys.

Introduction

Start by asking the children what they remember about the habitat they will be revisiting and the plants and animals living in the various habitats.

Explore their understanding of 'habitat' and of how living things depend on each other and the environment to live. Remind them of their work in Year 4 on identification and using keys — when they used two types of key to identify some invertebrates (they may have used a branching database program in addition).

Individual and group work

The children rehearse the skills involved in using a key, using Sheets 1, 2 or 3.

Whole class

Take the children through the process of making a key:

- Take four shells — cockle, mussel, razor shell and whelk. Make sure the bivalves are complete with both shells. Talk about the important features of each shell — whether there are one or two shells per animal — the colour, surface, shape.

- Then, choose a characteristic which only one of them has: only one shell, and you have the first question.

● Make up a second question which, again, only one of the three remaining shells has: a purplish-black shell. Carry on in this way until you have identified each type of shell — texture and shape of the shell. Where possible, add an extra question to make sure of each identification.

● Construct the key with the whole class, pointing out how the questions are designed to lead towards one physical feature that is unique to the animal and so to each organism.

Individual and group work.

Out in the field, ask the children to collect some things and make notes about others — collect invertebrates — spiders, beetles, centipedes, etc.; leaves from trees; or make notes about other organisms which may not be collected — birds, or flowers; for example, four blue, red or yellow flowers, noting the special features — number of petals, petal/leaf shape, seed head, position of the leaves, etc.

Back in the classroom, ask the children to identify their organisms from reference sources and then construct keys to help others to identify them. Use the obvious physical features and, if appropriate, information in the books to pull out differences between the organisms.

Whole class

Try out some of the children's keys with the class; encourage them to comment on each others' work.

Either at this stage in the lesson, or earlier, some children may attempt Sheet 4 using a key to identify amphibians and reptiles.

Differentiated Sc1 learning outcomes

Using keys to identify animals and plants

● uses a simple yes/no key for identifying organisms

● uses a simple branching key to identify four invertebrates

● uses a branching key to identify four skulls of small mammals

● uses a branching key of greater complexity to identify eight European amphibians and reptiles.

Making keys to identify plants and animals

● identifies several important differences between the organisms

● constructs questions with 'yes' or 'no' answers in a branching key which successfully identifies each organism

● knows about the organisation of invertebrates into groups through using a branching key to identify them.

Using the differentiated sheets

Sheet 1★★ asks the children to use a simple 'yes'/'no' key and a simple branching key to identify four different organisms — ant, worm, ladybird and spider. (Level 4)

Sheet 2★★ asks the children to use a simple branching key to identify four skulls of small mammals from an owl pellet. (Level 4)

Sheet 3★★★ asks the children to use a more complex branching key to identify eight amphibians and reptiles. (Level 4)

Sheet 4★★★ asks the children to use reference sources to distinguish between amphibians and reptiles using a key.

Sheet 5 is a record of learning for the children to fill in.

Background information

Using and making identification keys

A key consists of information arranged so that an unknown species can be identified. Most keys work by asking questions or matching pictures, to which the response is either 'yes' or 'no'. This either allows the organism to be identified or narrows down the choice through a branching key. Computer database keys are constructed on this principle.

Classification

The living world can be divided into five main groups or kingdoms. The two main ones are animals and plants and the three other kingdoms are simple organisms – bacteria, protists and fungi. In some methods of classification the simple organisms can be included in either of the main animal or plant groups.

Animals and plants are further divided into groups where all the members show strong likenesses to each other: animals are sub-divided into invertebrates and vertebrates, plants into those which do not have flowers and those which do. These are further divided into smaller and smaller classifications, the lowest of which is the species.

The process of classification continues to develop, as evolutionary relationships between organisms are clarified. Ideally, all the forms gathered together in one stage of classification have evolved from one ancestral species.

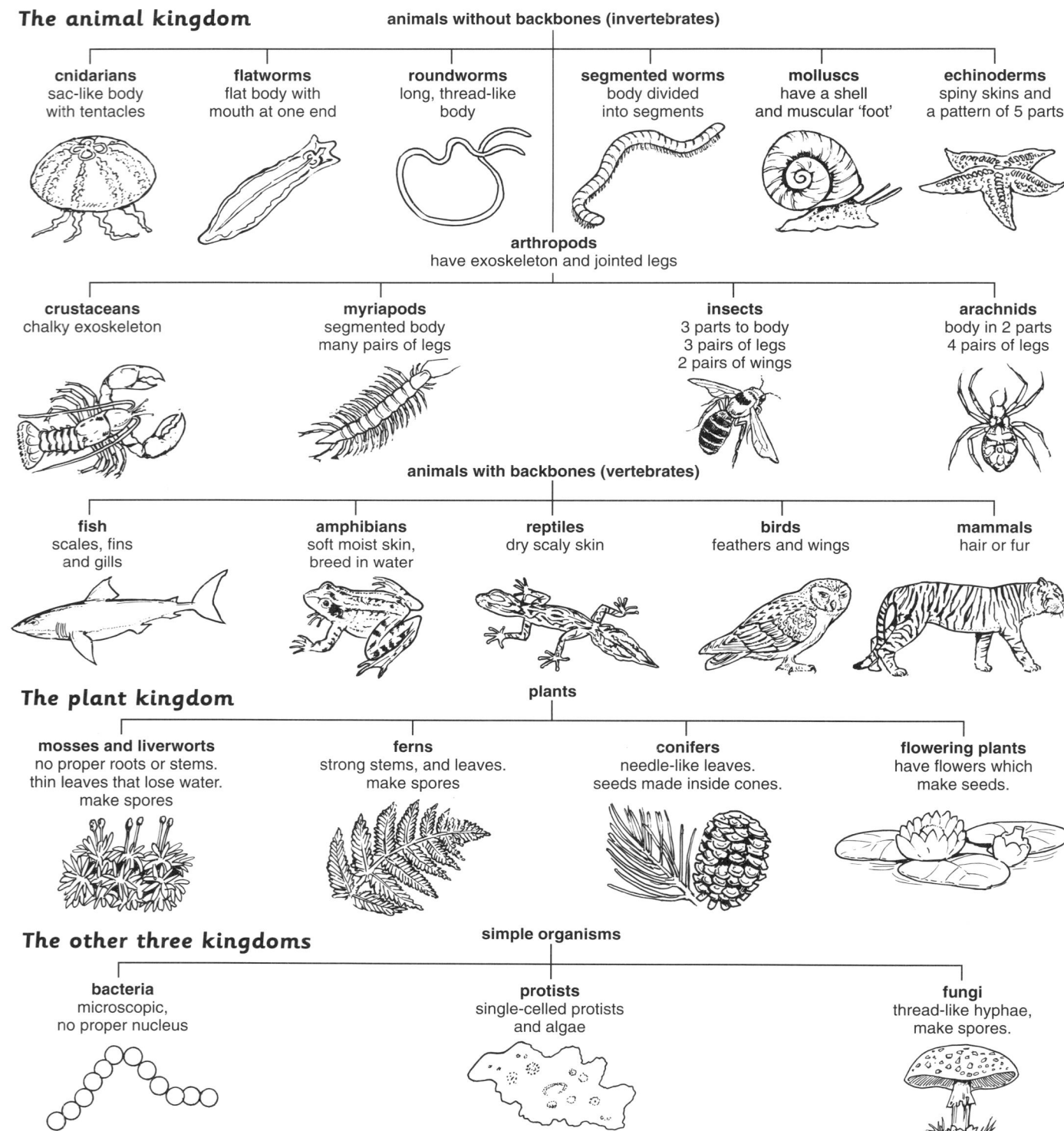

The animal kingdom

animals without backbones (invertebrates)

cnidarians
sac-like body
with tentacles

flatworms
flat body with
mouth at one end

roundworms
long, thread-like
body

segmented worms
body divided
into segments

molluscs
have a shell
and muscular 'foot'

echinoderms
spiny skins and
a pattern of 5 parts

arthropods
have exoskeleton and jointed legs

crustaceans
chalky exoskeleton

myriapods
segmented body
many pairs of legs

insects
3 parts to body
3 pairs of legs
2 pairs of wings

arachnids
body in 2 parts
4 pairs of legs

animals with backbones (vertebrates)

fish
scales, fins
and gills

amphibians
soft moist skin,
breed in water

reptiles
dry scaly skin

birds
feathers and wings

mammals
hair or fur

The plant kingdom

plants

mosses and liverworts
no proper roots or stems.
thin leaves that lose water.
make spores

ferns
strong stems, and leaves.
make spores

conifers
needle-like leaves.
seeds made inside cones.

flowering plants
have flowers which
make seeds.

The other three kingdoms

simple organisms

bacteria
microscopic,
no proper nucleus

protists
single-celled protists
and algae

fungi
thread-like hyphae,
make spores.

Name .... Date ....

Using keys to name invertebrates

Here are two different keys. Use them to name these animals:

Key 1

1. Does it have legs?
   No. It's an **earthworm**
   Yes. Go to 2.

2. Does it have eight legs?
   Yes. It's a **spider**
   No. Go to 3.

3. Does it have spots?
   Yes. It's a **ladybird**
   No. It's an **ant**.

A ....   B ....   C ....   D ....

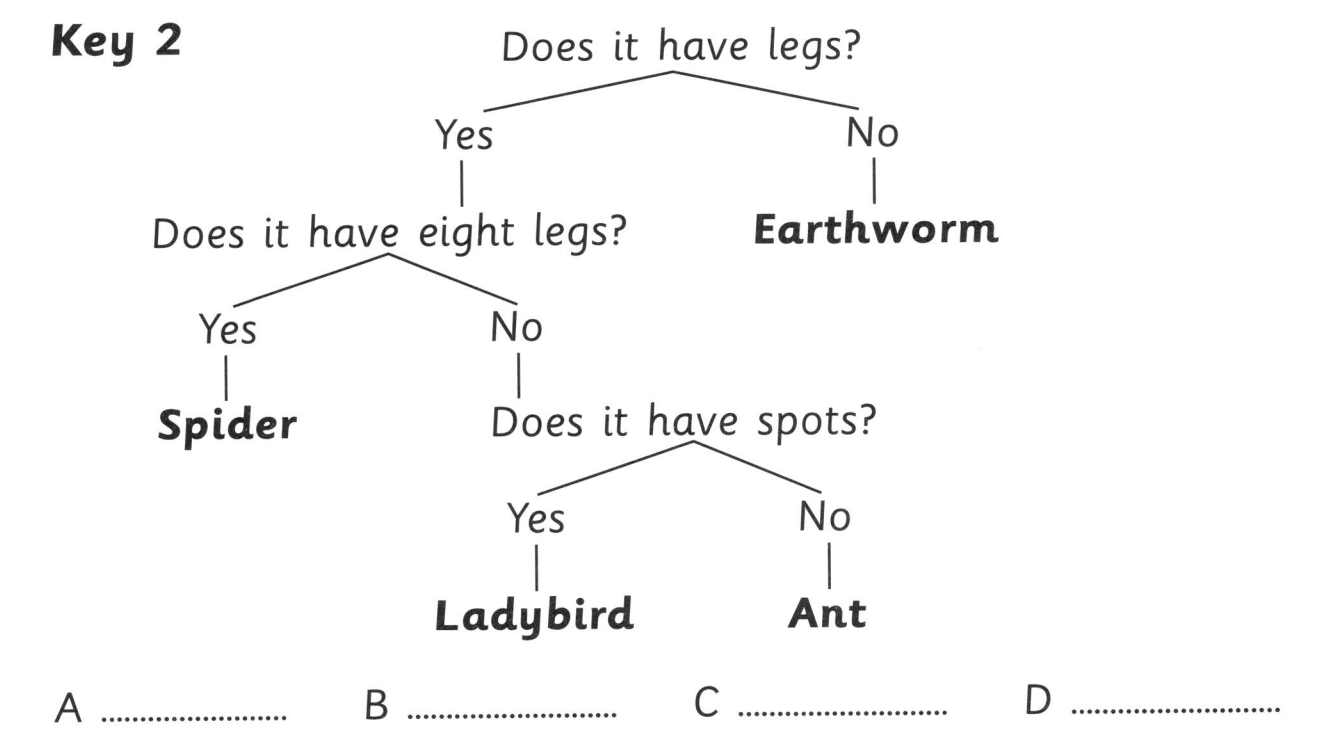

Key 2

Does it have legs?

Yes   No

Does it have eight legs?   **Earthworm**

Yes   No

Spider   Does it have spots?

Yes   No

Ladybird   **Ant**

A ....   B ....   C ....   D ....

Name .... Date ....

Using a key to identify animals owls eat

Owls eat small animals but cannot digest all parts of them. They regurgitate skulls, some bones and fur or feathers in owl pellets. Use the key to name the skulls found in some owl pellets.

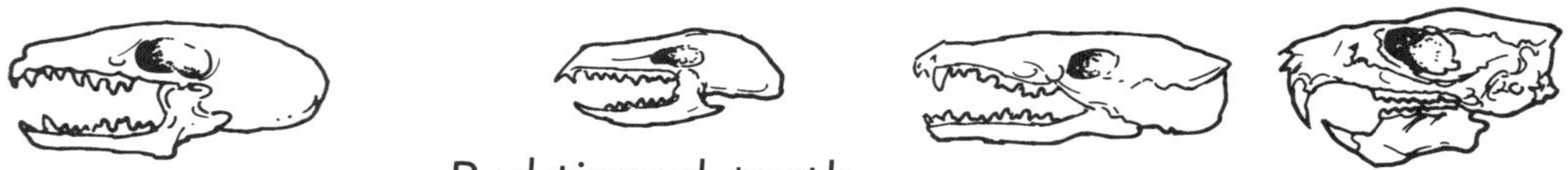

A   B   C   D

Red-tipped teeth

Does the skull have teeth?

Yes   No

Are the teeth evenly spaced   Does it have a beak?
with no gaps?

Yes   No   Yes

Does it have short incisors?   **Bird**

Yes   No

Mole   Does it have teeth   Is the top of the skull flat?
with red tips?

Yes   Yes   No

Shrew   **Rat**   **Rabbit**

Name .... Date ....

Using a key to identify some reptiles and amphibians

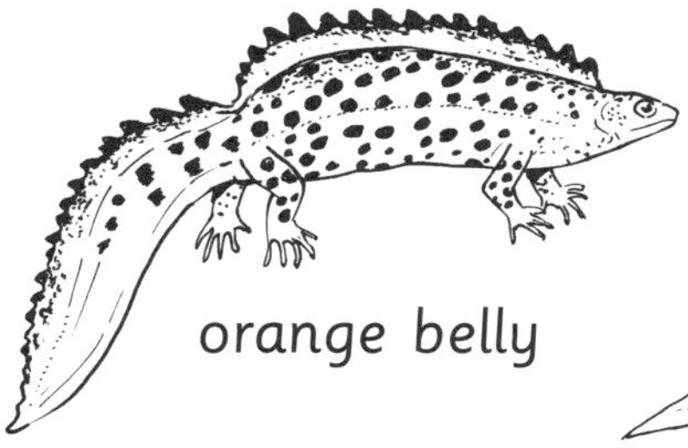

orange belly

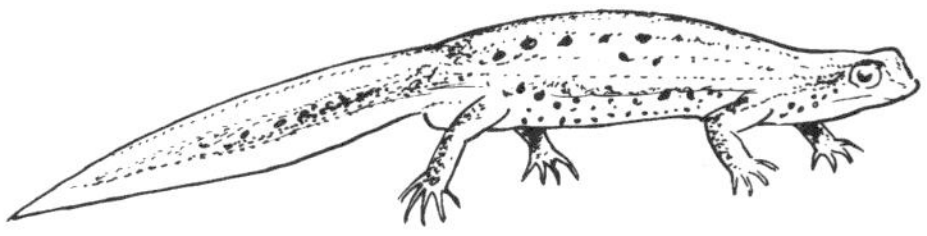

Does it have legs?

No

Yes

Zig-zag pattern down the back?

Big bulging eyes?

Yes

Yes

No

Adder

Bumpy warty skin?

Crest along back?

Yes

No

Yes

No

Common toad

Orange belly?

Webbed feet?

Smooth skin?

Yes

Yes

No

Yes

Crested newt

Palmate newt

Smooth newt

Common frog

Name .... Date ....

Amphibian or reptile?

Use reference sources and this key to find out:

Are they vertebrates?

Yes

Are they cold-blooded?

Yes

Do they have dry skin and scales or bony plates?

Yes   No

Do most lay their eggs on land or carry live young?   Do they have moist skin, mostly smooth, sometimes warty?

Yes   Yes

Reptiles   Do they lay their eggs in water?

eg Turtles, tortoises, snakes, lizards, crocodiles and alligators   Yes

Amphibians

eg Newts, frogs, toads

Write any other differences you found here: ....

....

....

....

Name .... Date ....

Interdependence and adaptation:
Using and making keys to identify organisms

Using keys to identify animals and plants

☐ I can use a simple yes/no key for identifying organisms

☐ I can use a simple branching key to identify four invertebrates

☐ I can use a branching key to identify four skulls of small mammals

☐ I can use a branching key to identify eight European amphibians and reptiles. (Level 4)

Making keys to identify plants and animals

☐ I can identify several important differences between the organisms

☐ I can construct questions with 'yes' or 'no' answers in a branching key that identifies each organism

☐ I know about the organisation of two vertebrate groups through using a branching key to identify the differences between them.

Micro-organisms:
What does yeast need to grow?

Nelson Thornes Ref: PS Kit 6.2.5

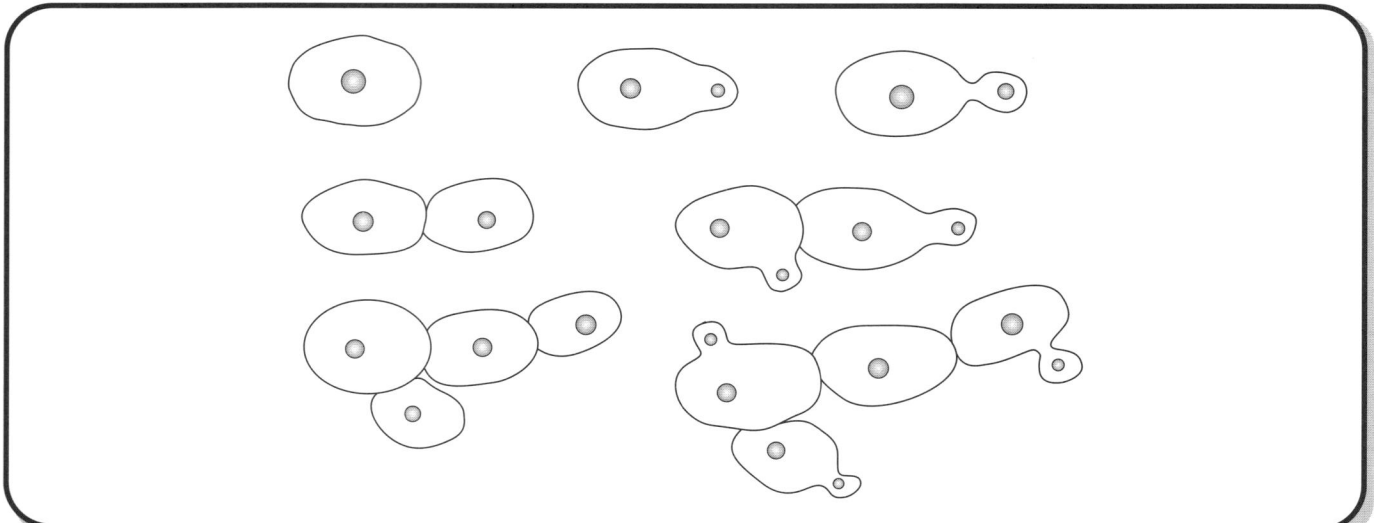

Learning objectives

Children should learn:

- that micro-organisms feed and grow
- to **make suggestions** about what yeast needs to grow
- to **make careful observations** and compare these in order **to draw conclusions** about the effect of yeast on dough
- to **explain conclusions using scientific knowledge and understanding**.

Lesson notes

 Approximate timing 2 hours

Prepare bread dough, some with and some without yeast, timed to finish rising around the start of the lesson. About half an hour before the lesson, make a mixture of yeast, sugar and warm water according to the instructions and leave it to activate.

Type of scientific enquiry

This Sc1 enquiry gives children the opportunity to plan and carry out a full investigation, including a fair test.

Introduction

Show the children some yeast in various forms — fresh, pelleted and powdered. Ask them what they know about it — what we use it for; explain what it is and how it reproduces. Ask if they think it is living.

Explain the main objective of the lesson — to find out what yeast needs to grow. Ask them to think about this as you show them the effect of yeast on the bread dough. Put it to bake. Without telling them what is in it, show them the mixture of yeast, water and sugar which is foaming nicely and explain that it is making new yeast cells and giving off a gas in the bubbles. This will help them to see what to expect, what their evidence will be. Ask how this shows that yeast is a living micro-organism.

Let the children read the instructions for using yeast on the various packets. Ask them to think about what plants need to grow or seeds need to germinate and to use these clues to suggest what yeast might need to grow.

Predictions — Yeast needs/does not need warmth/light/sugar to grow.

Questions which can be tested:

1. Does yeast need light to grow?
2. Does sugar make yeast grow?
3. Does temperature affect how well yeast grows?

Predictions —
If we keep yeast in the dark, it will not grow because plants need light to grow well.

Yeast with sugar will grow, but not without sugar because sugar is food and all living things need food.

Yeast will grow in warm water but not in cold or hot water. I think this is because organisms need some warmth to grow but not too much.

Individual and group work

The children plan fair tests to answer their question. To provide corroborating evidence, ensure that more than one pair or small group does each investigation.

Use Sheets 1 to 4. For tests 1 and 2 above, put the mixture in a clear beaker and watch for a foam forming on the top — the more foam, the more growth.

For test 3, some children could try putting the mixtures into small, clear, drinks bottles with well-stretched balloons over the neck. These will inflate slightly as the gas produced by the yeast increases. In this test, use water at three different temperatures — cold, 5°C or less; warm, about 37°C; and hot, above 60°C. Leave them for about 20 minutes to half an hour in a temperature of about 23°C or according to the instructions. (The yeast will go on producing bubbles for much longer than this if required.)

 If the gas is produced quickly, ease the balloon slightly to prevent it blowing off.

The children watch what happens, observing carefully, looking for changes in the mixtures and using all appropriate senses. They have an opportunity to write freely about their observations. Discuss the children's ideas about what is happening and what it means.

The children interpret their findings and draw conclusions. If appropriate, leave the explanations for later.

At convenient times, show them the texture of the baked bread and explain how the holes are made. Some of the children may look at yeast growing under a binocular microscope on 8×–10× magnification.

Whole class

Discuss each aspect of the investigations. Begin with their predictions — were they valid? Ask individuals to describe their test and results, encourage the children to ask each other questions and where appropriate, corroborate or challenge their results. Discuss the basis for their conclusions; work towards generalisations — yeast needs sugar (food) and warmth to grow, it does not need light. Ask the children to try to explain verbally what is happening — yeast grows and reproduces when it has sugar/warmth/both sugar and warmth. Living things grow, excrete and reproduce, so this shows that yeast

is living. Ask them to think carefully about their explanations, discuss them and record them on Sheets 2 to 4.

Differentiated Sc1 learning outcomes

Making suggestions about what yeast needs to grow

● puts forward their own idea

● makes a prediction based on knowledge about what plants and/or animals need to grow (uses scientific knowledge)

● predicts that yeast needs food (sugar) and warmth to grow.

Observing

● makes use of several senses

● notices relevant details, identifying similarities and differences

● discerns the order in which events take place.

Drawing conclusions

● interprets results by linking events together

● identifies a pattern in their observations

● ensures that the pattern or association is checked against all the data

● shows caution in making assumptions about their conclusion

● draws a valid conclusion from their evidence.

Explaining

● makes a statement of the circumstances — yeast does not need light to grow

● links cause and effect in an explanation — the sugar helped the yeast to grow; some heat is necessary for the yeast to grow well

● offers an explanation involving an applied principle — sugar helped the yeast to grow because it is their food.

Using the differentiated sheets

Sheet 1★★ gives the children practice in predicting, observing and drawing conclusions. (Level 3/4)

Sheet 2★★ gives the children a full outline to plan and carry out an investigation. (Level 4)

Sheet 3★★★ gives the children an outline with fewer details and more decisions to make (Level 4)

Sheet 4★★★ gives the children the opportunity for extended writing within a suggested framework. (Level 5)

Sheet 5 is a sheet for children to record their Sc1 skills in this investigation.

Background information

Making suggestions about what yeast needs to grow

Behind every prediction is some previous knowledge about the answer to the question. At this stage, the children are becoming better at using their scientific and everyday knowledge about how things behave. For example, in this investigation, the children will know some of the needs of all living things, such as food, and of some living things, light, warmth. If they also read the instructions about how to use yeast, they will see that sugar is needed, so they will link the two ideas and suggest that yeast needs sugar, perhaps adding 'as food to make it grow'. Their past experience with predicting and encouragement from the teacher will suggest that assumptions should be made with caution; the pattern may not apply in this case (and that is why they are doing the test). They should also be able to distinguish a prediction from a guess, which cannot be justified in terms of the evidence of previous learning.

Observing

Using the appropriate senses to note details and make comparisons between objects is something most children enjoy and are good at. To observe events, noting changes, differences and the order in which the events occur, are important skills they will be developing at this stage. This is 'observation in action' — involving careful observation.

Interpreting findings

This involves putting results together so that patterns or relationships between them can be seen. Questions such as — Does yeast need light to grow? Does yeast need sugar to grow? Does warmth affect how well yeast grows? — contain the factors involved and indicate where to look for patterns and relationships.

Drawing a general conclusion or generalisation from the evidence needs care, because it could suggest that this relationship is not only found in this particular investigation, but would be true in other cases, too. So the children will need corroborative evidence from others' tests and their knowledge of the uses we make of yeast in bread, beer and wine. It is important to check a pattern against all available evidence.

Drawing a conclusion on the effect of heat on the rate of growth of yeast is justified only if there are at least three different conditions — cold, warm and hot.

Explaining

In science the term 'explaining' does not imply certainty. Scientific knowledge is tentative, open to contradiction and/or development. Children's explanations are best offered in such an atmosphere — as suggestions, attempts, leaps of the imagination, incomplete offerings that attempt to suggest how things are as they are. A useful explanation links cause and effect and explores how a general principle applies in the circumstances.

Yeast

Yeasts are single-celled, microscopic fungi found in all parts of the world in the soil and in organic matter. For example, they occur naturally as a white covering (a bloom) on grapes and other fruit. They are produced commercially for use in baking, brewing and wine-making. They grow and reproduce by 'budding', where an outgrowth from a cell enlarges, separates from the parent and lives independently. Sometimes clusters of attached cells can be seen under a microscope. Yeast needs food and water to grow. Enzymes in the yeast break down sugar into carbon dioxide and alcohol (ethanol) in the absence of oxygen, which makes energy available for their life processes. This is called anaerobic respiration.

In baking, yeast is used to make the dough 'rise' as a result of the carbon dioxide bubbles (which are tasteless and harmless) given off before the bread is baked. The heat kills the yeast, leaving the bubbles held in place by the gluten in the flour. They expand in the heat of the oven.

Name .... Date ....

Investigating yeast

1. A Fair test

Some children asked — Does yeast need sugar to grow?

Group 1 planned like this:

We changed: *the sugar, the temperature*
We kept the same: *the amount of water and the amount of yeast*
We observed: *changes in the mixture*

Group 2 planned like this:

We changed: *the sugar*
We kept the same: *the amount and temperature of the water and the amount of yeast*
We observed: *changes in the mixture*

Which one is not a fair test? Say why you think so.

....

2. Here are the results from the group that did a fair test:

*A foam came on the top of the beaker of yeast, water and sugar.
There was no foam in the beaker without sugar.*

One group concluded that: 'Yeast makes a foam when it grows. The beaker with foam has sugar in it. The beaker with no sugar has no foam, so the yeast is not growing. So yeast needs sugar to grow.'
But another group said 'Yeast can't grow, it is not living. The bubbles are from the sugar in the warm water.'

Which one is correct? Say why you think so.

....

....

3. Tick the evidence the group should use to draw a conclusion.

☐ The results of their test
☐ The results of other groups' tests
☐ What the instructions on the packets of yeast say
☐ The results of another test on just sugar and water
☐ All of these.

Give a reason. ....

....

Name .... Date ....

Investigating yeast

My question is: ....

(Check — is it a question that you can test?)

I predict that: ....

because ....

This is a fair test.

I changed ....

I kept these the same: ....

I observed ....

(Check — have you only changed one factor and kept others the same?)

This is what I observed happening: ....

....

....

(Check — have you looked several times and written down the order in which things happened?)

This is what the results mean: ....

....

(Check — have you made a link between what happened and what you changed?)

My conclusion: ....

(Check — have you used evidence from other children's tests to make your conclusion better?)

My explanation: ....

....

(Check — have you thought about what you know already about living things to help you explain?)

Name .... Date ....

Investigating yeast

Question: ....

Prediction: ....

Fair test

What we change	What we keep the same	What we observe

Observations: ....

....

....

Results: ....

What the results mean: ....

....

Conclusion: ....

Explanation: ....

....

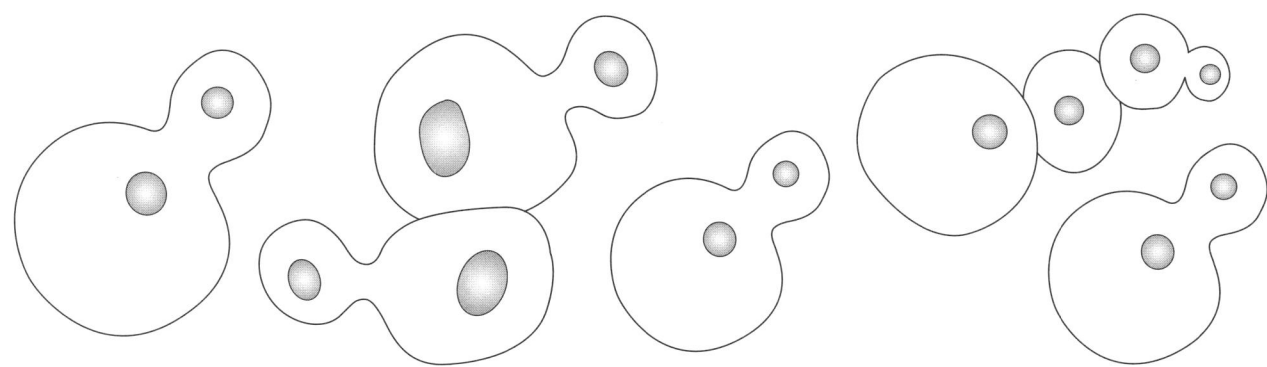

Name .... Date ....

Investigating yeast

Does yeast need warmth to grow?

Together with your partner, write about your investigation.

Include these sub-headings:

Planning — your prediction, fair test and equipment.

Observations — results showing what happened

Conclusion

What the results mean.

Explanation (you could leave this until after the whole class discussion).

Record your investigation on another sheet of paper.

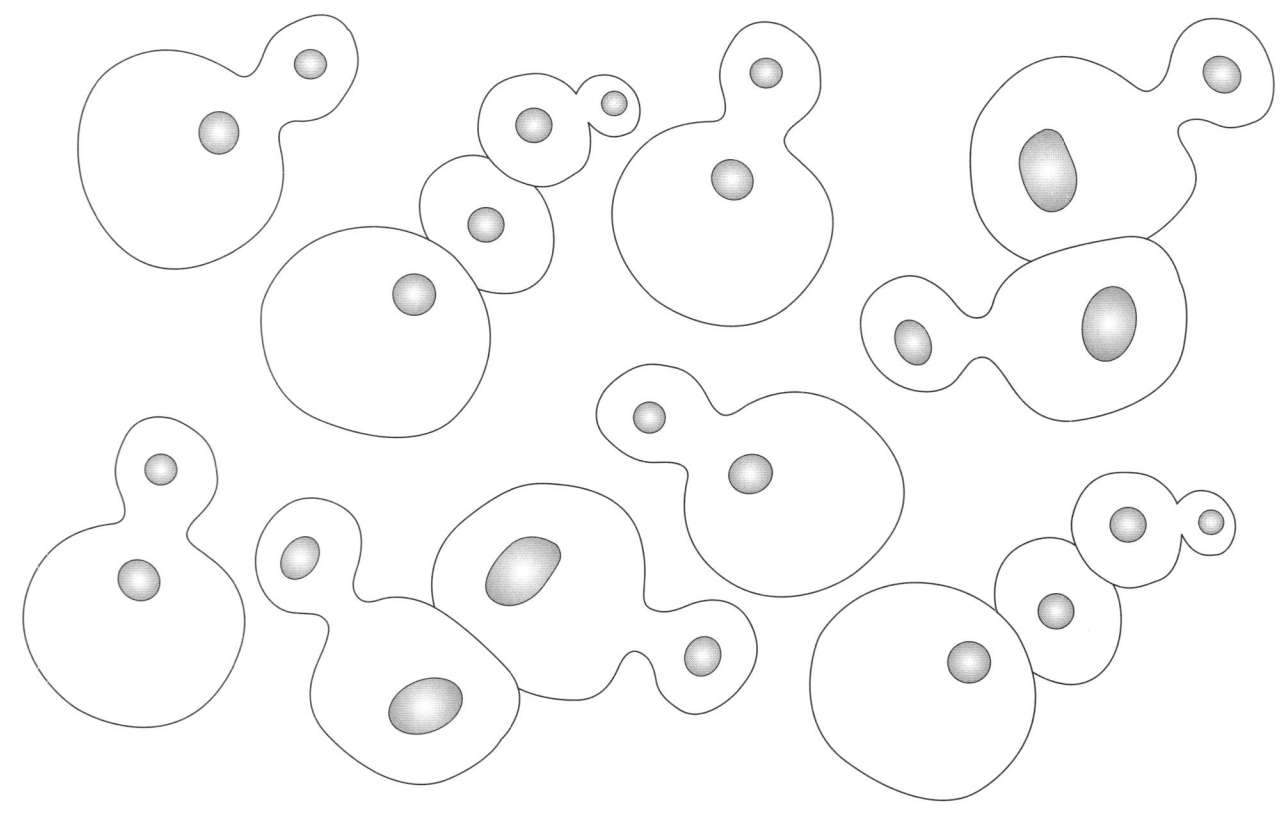

Name .... Date ....

What does yeast need to grow?

Making suggestions about what yeast needs to grow

❏ I suggested my own idea. (Level 4)

❏ I made a prediction based on what I know about plants' and animals' needs. (Level 5)

❏ I predicted that yeast needs food (sugar) and warmth to grow. (Level 5)

Observing

❏ I noticed important details, and identified similarities and differences. (Level 5)

❏ I made notes about the order the events took place.

Drawing conclusions

❏ I linked events together.

❏ I identified a pattern in my observations. (Level 4)

❏ I checked the pattern against all the data. (Level 5)

❏ I was careful about not jumping to conclusions.

❏ I drew a valid conclusion from my evidence. (Level 5)

More about dissolving:
What affects how quickly sugar dissolves?

Nelson Thornes Ref: PS Kit 6.3.4

Learning objectives

Children should learn:

● to **turn ideas about helping solids dissolve more quickly into a form that can be investigated and decide how to carry out a fair test**

● to **decide what apparatus to use and to make careful observations and measurements**

● to **use a line graph or bar chart to present results**

● to **make comparisons and draw conclusions**.

Lesson notes

 Approximate timing: 2 hours

Type of scientific enquiry

This Sc1 enquiry will give children the opportunity to tackle a whole investigation based on fair testing.

Introduction

Add a spoonful of sugar to a mug of coffee and stir. Ask who takes sugar in tea or coffee. Then pose the question 'What might affect how quickly the sugar dissolves?'

Record a list of factors (which will all be potential starting points for investigations).

Choose one factor to illustrate the need to vary one factor whilst keeping others the same to construct a fair test. (Sheet 1)

Group work

Assign different groups to investigate different factors. Bear in mind that those investigating the effect of a continuous variable, such as temperature, can present results on line graphs (characteristic of Level 5 — see Sheet 3) whereas those investigating a categoric variable, such as type of sugar, will produce bar charts (characteristic of Level 4 — see Sheet 2).

Point out the difficulty we have in measuring the time for sugar to dissolve accurately (and controlling the rate of stirring) and how repeating timings will improve the reliability of our results.

Present results from their tables as bar charts or line graphs as appropriate.

Whole class

Draw together the results of the various factors investigated to gain an overview of the factors that affect sugar dissolving.

Evaluate the difficulties in performing the tests and how to improve the confidence we can have in any conclusions we draw.

Differentiated Sc1 learning outcomes

Planning

- with help, decides what to change, what to measure and what to keep the same
- decides what to change, what to measure and what to keep the same
- decides what to change, what to measure and what to keep the same and selects apparatus to use themselves.

Recording

- with help, fills in a table of results and displays them on a bar chart
- fills in a table of results and displays them on a bar chart
- designs and fills in a table of results and displays them on a line graph.

Concluding

- uses measurements to sequence the results of their tests
- uses their bar chart to sequence the results of their tests
- uses their line graph to describe the pattern in their results and puts forward their own ideas to explain why they think this happens.

Using the differentiated sheets

Sheet 1★★ This sheet gives access to Level 5 skills (listing key factors), but does provide children with the dependent variable, the factor they will measure, which can be confusing in an investigation which involves lots of measuring. (Level 4)

Sheet 2★ This sheet supports recording for those investigating different types of sugar and asks the children to sequence their results. (Level 2/3)

Sheet 3★★★ This sheet helps children record the results of repeat readings in an extended investigation looking at the effect of temperature on the rate of dissolving. They then draw a line graph and comment on the pattern obtained. (Level 5)

Sheet 4★★ This Skill Sheet requires children to process results on to a bar chart then sequence the order of dissolving. (Level 4)

Sheet 5★★★ This Skill Sheet requires children to process repeat readings, displaying them on a line graph and to comment on the pattern. (Level 5)

Sheet 6 This is the pupil record sheet to complete for this enquiry.

Background information

Planning

Given a planning frame, most children will be able to think of factors that affect dissolving and choose one to investigate, keeping the others the same in their fair test.

A few trial runs will help children choose values for the mass of sugar and volume of water they use in each test. It will also give a chance for children to see how difficult it is to judge the exact time it takes sugar to dissolve, and the higher attaining children will plan to take repeat measurements.

Measuring

This investigation is a good chance to teach children about taking measurements with an appropriate degree of accuracy for the task at hand. Although electronic stop-watches will read times to the nearest one hundredth of a second, we cannot judge the exact moment when the solid has completely dissolved that precisely. Stop-clocks are perfectly adequate for this task.

This difficulty in making precise measurements also presents a good opportunity to demonstrate why it gives us more reliable data to repeat measurements in some enquiries.

Recording

Most children will now be making a good attempt at designing their own tables, with the higher attaining children producing tables for their repeat measurements.

The graphs produced will depend on the variable under investigation. The higher attaining children should be encouraged to look at the effect of a continuous variable (one that is measured) and display their results on a line graph. Those working towards Level 4 can look at different types of sugar and go on to produce a bar chart.

Concluding

Children should be looking for patterns in their graphs and should be making generalisations linking the effects of one variable on the other. For example, the higher the temperature, the more quickly the sugar dissolves. They should be encouraged to look in more detail at the shape of any line graphs and to comment on variations in its slope.

● Does changing the temperature have a greater effect at lower or higher temperatures?

● How does your graph tell you that?

Dissolving

When a substance dissolves in water its particles (molecules in the case of sugar, or ions — charged particles — in the case of salt) become dispersed throughout the solution. Water molecules are attracted to the particles in a soluble solid which are 'pulled away' from their neighbouring particles. The dissolved particles become surrounded by water molecules as the solution forms.

Increasing the surface area of the solid will expose more of its particles to the attraction of water molecules. At higher temperatures the water molecules possess more energy, and their increased movement will aid the breakdown of the solid's structure, increasing the rate of dissolving.

Name .... Date ....

What affects how quickly sugar dissolves?

List all the factors that you think might affect how quickly sugar dissolves:

....

....

....

In our test we plan to see how .... affects how quickly sugar dissolves.

We will change:

We will measure: | The time it takes for the sugar to dissolve in water |

We will keep these things the same: ....

....

....

Name .... Date ....

What affects how quickly sugar dissolves?

Results

Type of sugar tested	Time to dissolve (seconds)

Draw a bar chart to display your results.

My conclusion

From my results I can put the sugar we tested into this order:

1. .... (dissolved most quickly)

2. ....

3. ....

4. ....

Name .... Date ....

What affects how quickly sugar dissolves?

Results

Temperature of water (°C)	Time for sugar to dissolve (s)			
	1st test	2nd test	3rd test	Mean

Graph to show how temperature affects the time taken to dissolve

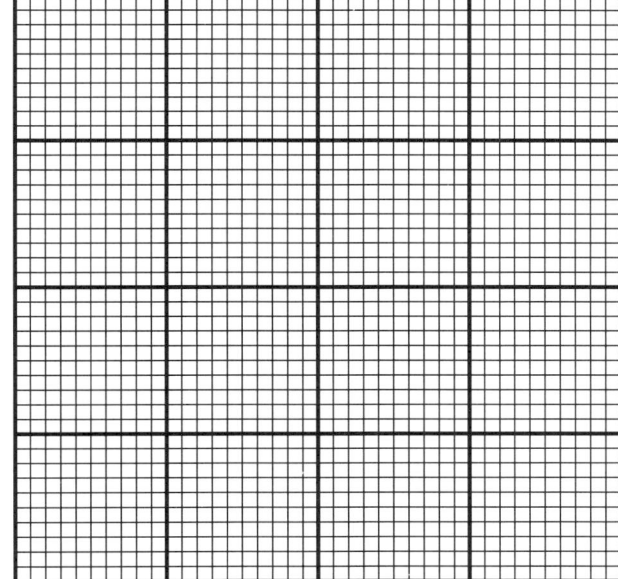

Conclusion

From my graph I can say that ....

....

....

....

Name .... Date ....

What affects how quickly sugar dissolves?

A group timed how long it takes for different types of sugar to dissolve.

Here are the results of their test:

Type of sugar	Time to dissolve (seconds)
Cube	200
Brown	150
Icing	25
Granulated	45

a) Draw a bar chart to show their results on a piece of graph paper.

b) Put the types of sugar into order:

1. .... (dissolves most quickly)

2. ....

3. ....

4. ....

Name .... Date ....

How does temperature affect how quickly sugar dissolves?

A group were investigating how temperature affects the time it takes sugar to dissolve.

Here are the results of their tests:

Temperature of water (°C)	Time for sugar to dissolve (s)			
	1st test	2nd test	3rd test	Mean
20	298	227	237	
30	121	143	138	
40	52	65	78	
50	39	55	37	

a) Work out the mean of the test results to fill in the last column of the table above.

b) Draw a line graph to show the results.

c) How does temperature affect the time it takes sugar to dissolve?

....

....

Name .... Date ....

What affects how quickly sugar dissolves?

Planning

☐ With help, I can plan what to change, what to measure and what to keep the same to carry out a fair test. (Level 3)

☐ I can plan what to change, what to measure and what to keep the same to carry out a fair test. (Level 4)

☐ I can list the key factors and plan what to change, what to measure and what to keep the same to carry out a fair test. (Level 5)

Concluding

☐ I can put the different types of sugar into order based on how quickly they dissolve. (Level 2)

☐ I can put the different types of sugar into order based on how quickly they dissolve, and explain how I decided on the order from my results. (Level 3)

☐ I can put the different types of sugar into order based on how quickly they dissolve, and explain why we get this order using scientific ideas. (Level 4)

☐ I can state the pattern from my line graph, and explain why we get this pattern using scientific ideas. (Level 5)

Forces in action:
What affects how quickly a spinner falls?

Nelson Thornes Ref: PS Kit 6.5.8

Learning objectives

Children should learn:

● that air resistance slows moving objects

● that when an object falls, air resistance acts in the opposite direction to the weight

● to **check measurements by repeating them**

● to **interpret a line graph** and use it to describe the motion of spinners falling.

Lesson notes

 Approximate timing: 2 hours

Type of scientific enquiry

This Sc1 enquiry will give children the opportunity to tackle a whole investigation based on fair testing.

Introduction

If possible show the class a sycamore seed falling. After a brief discussion tell the class that they are going to investigate the factors that affect how quickly a paper spinner falls. Have a paper spinner already made up and a template to show children. Ask them to generate a list of factors that might matter in their groups. (Sheet 1).

Group work

Children can investigate one of the factors they identify, using stop watches that read to one hundredth of a second. Groups will be looking at the effect of varying the number of paper clips, the

height they drop the spinner from, the length of the wings, etc. This offers another opportunity to reinforce the need to repeat readings when accurate measurement is difficult. Sheet 3 offers a format for recording repeat readings.

Groups should record their results in tables and then display them on appropriate graphs (Sheets 2 and 3).

Whole class

Look at the results from different groups, stressing pattern recognition from their graphs and explanation of the pattern using their prior knowledge of gravity and air resistance. Sheet 4 provides a framework to record children's conclusions, plus a section for evaluation.

Differentiated learning outcomes for Sc1

Planning

● With help, decides what to change, what to measure and what to keep the same

● decides what to change, what to measure and what to keep the same.

Recording

● With help, fills in a table of results and displays them on a graph

● fills in a table of results and displays them on a graph

● designs and fills in a table of results to cater for repeat measurements and displays results on a graph.

Concluding

● Uses measurements to sequence the results of their tests

● uses their graph to sequence the results of their tests

● uses their graph to describe the pattern in their results and puts forward their own ideas to explain why they think this happens.

Using the differentiated sheets

Sheet 1★★ This sheet gives access to Level 5 skills (listing key factors), but does provide children with the dependent variable, the factor they will measure, which can be confusing in an investigation which involves lots of other measuring. (Level 4)

Sheet 2★★ This sheet supports recording results, with children filling in the independent variable (the factor they change) and asks the children to graph their results and draw a conclusion. (Level 4/5)

Sheet 3★★★ This sheet helps children record the results of repeat readings. They then draw a graph. (Level 5)

Sheet 4★★ This sheet structures the conclusion and evaluation and can be used in conjunction with Sheet 3. (Level 4/5)

Sheet 5★★★ This Skill Sheet requires children to process repeat readings, displaying them on a line graph, to comment on the pattern, and to explain the differences in repeat readings. (Level 5)

Sheet 6 This is the pupil record sheet to complete for this enquiry.

Background information

Measuring

In this investigation we need timers that will read as precisely as possible because the time intervals are so short. However, most children will appreciate the inherent inaccuracy in making such measurements by hand. The need for repeat measurements is accepted readily by children.

Some will need support in reading stop-watches and recording the decimal numbers involved.

Recording

The small numbers and measurements taken to two decimal places will mean that many children will need support in presenting their results on a line graph. Most children will need help with scaling up the vertical axis is difficult and plotting points.

Concluding

The graphs produced should be used to interpret the link between the two variables. Again stress the language of pattern recognition. For example, the bigger the wings, the slower the spinner falls.

Encourage deeper thinking about the pattern by asking questions such as, 'Is that always true? What happens if the wings are really big? Try one out!'

The use of their previous work on forces and friction should be used to explain any patterns they see in their results.

Air resistance

As an object moves through air, it will experience a force in the opposite direction to its movement. This 'air resistance' is due to collisions with the molecules of gas in the air. Large, flat surfaces at right angles to the movement of the object will be hit by more air molecules and will experience greater air resistance than smooth, streamlined shapes that 'cut through' the air more effectively.

Much research takes place in the transport industry to reduce air resistance and its associated reduction in fuel consumption at any given speed.

Name .... Date ....

What affects how quickly a spinner falls?

List all the factors that you think might affect how quickly a spinner falls:

....

....

....

In our test we plan to see how .... affects how quickly a spinner falls.

We will change:

We will measure:

The time it takes for the spinner to hit the floor

We will keep these things the same: ....

....

....

Name .... Date ....

What affects how quickly a spinner falls?

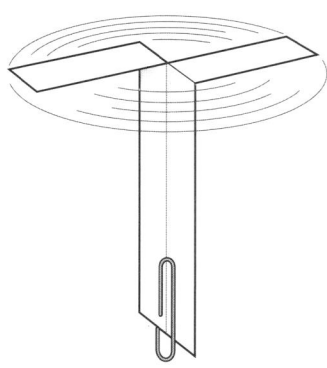

Results

Fill in the factor you are investigating at the top of the first column in the table below:

	Time to fall (seconds)

Draw a graph to display your results.

My conclusion

From my results I can say that ....

....

....

Name .... Date ....

What affects how quickly a spinner falls?

Results

Fill in the factor you are investigating at the top of the first column in the table below:

| | Time for spinner to fall (seconds) | | | |
	1st test	2nd test	3rd test	Mean

Now draw a graph to show your results.

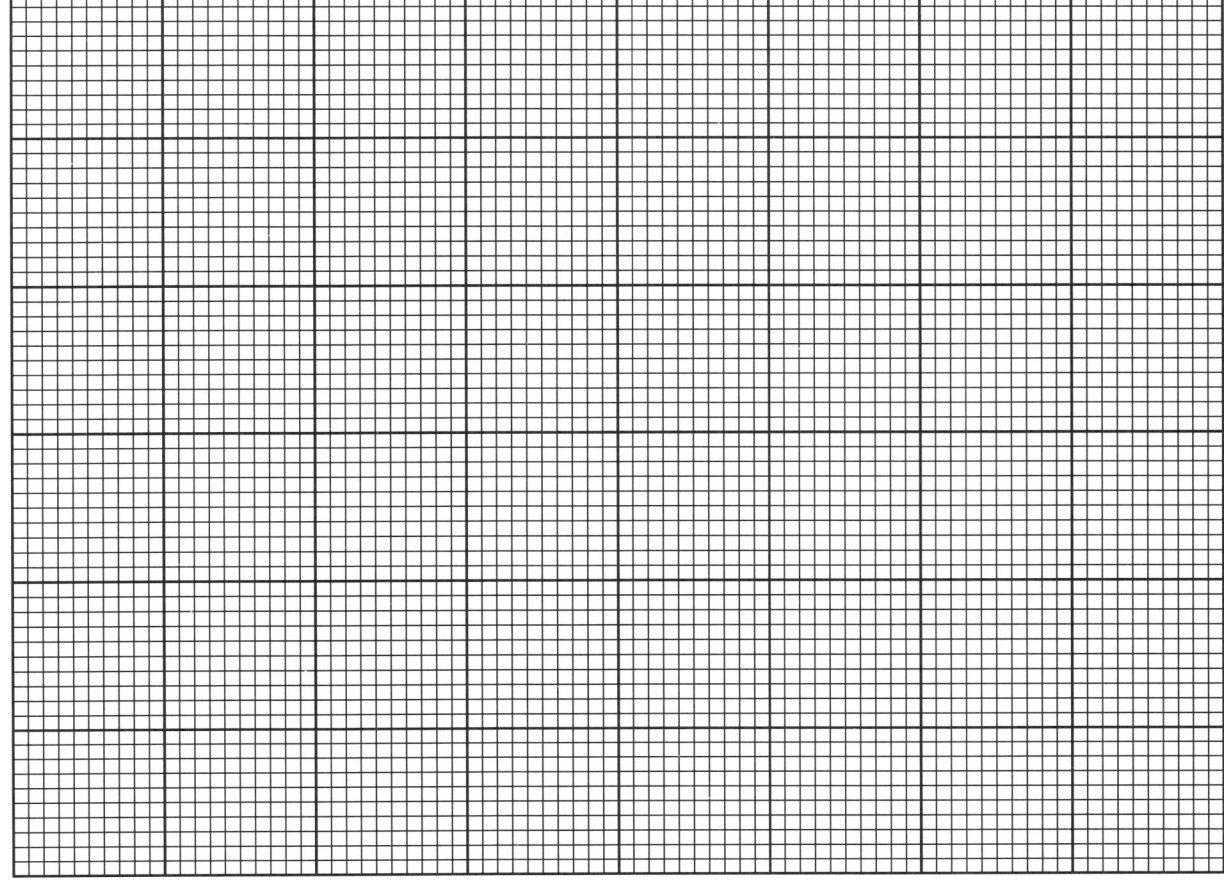

Name .... Date ....

What affects how quickly a spinner falls?

Conclusion

From my graph, the pattern is ....

....

Use the diagram below to explain why you get this pattern in your results.

Draw arrows and label them to describe the forces on the spinner.

Evaluation

These were the problems we had while doing our investigation:

....

....

....

How could you improve your investigation?

....

....

....

Name .... Date ....

How does height affect how quickly a spinner falls?

A group were investigating how the height you drop a spinner from affects the time it takes to fall.

Here are the results of their tests:

Height spinner is dropped from (m)	Time for spinner to hit the floor (s)			
	1st test	2nd test	3rd test	Mean
1.0	1.89	1.86	1.53	
1.5	2.57	2.23	2.28	
2.0	3.53	3.20	2.99	
2.5	4.16	3.66	3.93	

a) Work out the mean of the test results to fill in the last column of the table above.

b) Draw a line graph to show the results.

c) How does the height you drop a spinner from affect the time it takes to fall? ....

....

d) Suggest a reason why there are differences in timings taken at any one height.

....

....

Name .... Date ....

What affects how quickly a spinner falls?

Measuring

❏ I can measure the height we drop the spinners from. (Level 3)

❏ I can measure the height we drop the spinners from and time how long it takes to hit the floor when my partner lets it go. (Level 4)

❏ I know why it is better to take repeat readings in this investigation and can work out mean times to get more reliable results. (Level 5)

Concluding

❏ I can say which spinner fell most quickly. (Level 2)

❏ I can put the spinners into order based on how quickly they fall, and explain how I decided on the order from my results. (Level 3)

❏ I can put the spinners into order based on how quickly they fall, and explain why we get this order using scientific ideas. (Level 4)

❏ I can state the pattern from my line graph, and explain why we get this pattern using scientific ideas about forces and air resistance. (Level 5)